"I, who have never stopped looking for answers to the "why" of Harry's suicide even after more than 25 years since his death, raced through these pages with nods of recognition and pauses of gratitude for my deeper knowledge of the unique circumstances that influence the suicide of a physician, including that of my husband."

Carla Fine, author, *No Time to Say Goodbye:*
Surviving the Suicide of a Loved One

"This is a signature book for physicians, their families, those who train them and those who treat them. In tackling one of the biggest medical challenges of our time – physician depression and suicide, Dr. Myers has combined his lifelong clinical experience as a "doctors' doctor" with gripping anecdotes of families who have lost a physician loved one to suicide. By vividly, describing the context, the culture of medicine, the impact of stigma and through the use of compelling personal narratives, Dr Myers has opened the door to a topic that has been hidden in the shadows of shame and silence for decades. In addition to describing the problem, Dr. Myers offers practical solutions and reminds us all that we can make a difference in the lives of our patients and those we love."

Carol A. Bernstein, MD, Associate Professor of Psychiatry,
Vice Chair for Education and Director of Residency Training,
New York University School of Medicine,
Past President, American Psychiatric Association

"There could not be a more timely and informative piece of work on the topic of physician suicide. While public attitudes are opening up to the importance of a proactive approach to mental health, physicians continue to take their lives at a rate higher than the general population. With hard earned compassion and insight, Dr. Myers guides the reader through the many aspects that contribute to physician suicide. Using a broad ranging lens to examine the reasons for the increased risk among physicians, including science, history, and cultural perspectives, the most valuable lens is the vast depth of Dr. Myers' experience based on decades of working with physicians with mental health problems and who have struggled or tragically succumbed to suicide. Using personal narrative, and case examples alongside a scholarly approach, the effect is a readable, moving and critically important resource for medical educators and anyone who is touched by physician suicide."

Christine Moutier, MD, Chief Medical Officer,
American Foundation for Suicide Prevention

WHY
PHYSICIANS
DIE BY
SUICIDE

Other books by Michael F. Myers, MD

The Physician as Patient: A Clinical Handbook for Mental Health Professionals (with Glen O Gabbard, MD)

Touched by Suicide: Hope and Healing After Loss (with Carla Fine)

Intimate Relationships in Medical School: How to Make Them Work

How's Your Marriage? A Book for Men and Women

Doctors' Marriages: A Look at the Problems and Their Solutions

WHY PHYSICIANS DIE BY SUICIDE

LESSONS LEARNED FROM THEIR FAMILIES
AND OTHERS WHO CARED

MICHAEL F. MYERS, MD

www.michaelfmyers.com

Printed in the United States of America.

ISBN: 978-0-6928318-7-8

Book design: Dean Fetzer, www.gunboss.com

CONTENTS

*"...any man's death diminishes me, because
I am involved in Mankinde..."*

John Donne, Meditation XVII "No Man Is an Island."

DEDICATION

In honor of my medical school roommate Bill and all other medical students and physicians who have gone down that road, I offer this book.

NOTE

There are many quotes in this book. I have used the term "pseudonym" in most cases. However, there are other times when the name given is disguised to protect the individual's privacy. In situations where the actual person's name is written, the individual has signed a release granting permission for that to occur.

Also, rather than use the cumbersome gender expression "he or she" repeatedly, I have arbitrarily and alternately used male and female gender pronouns in the service of stylistic flow and progression.

FOREWORD

My husband, Harry Reiss, a prominent New York doctor, killed himself on December 16, 1989 at the age of 43. We were married for 21 years and I had accompanied him on the long and arduous journey through medical school, internship, residency, fellowship, and establishing a successful solo private practice as a board-certified urologist in Manhattan. At the prime of his life and his career, Harry injected himself with a lethal dose of the anesthetic Thiopental. I found him dead in his medical office when he was late coming home and I could not reach him.

Suicide is not spoken about openly or easily, especially in the medical community. There is a wall of silence surrounding this mysterious topic, probably because the pain is so private and the act so public. But now, luckily, we have this profoundly insightful book written by Dr. Michael Myers, a distinguished psychiatrist who has been treating physicians and their families for his entire illustrious career. I, who have never stopped looking for answers to the "why" of Harry's suicide even after more than 25 years since his death, raced through these pages with nods of recognition and pauses of gratitude for my deeper knowledge of the unique circumstances that influence the suicide of a physician, including that of my husband.

In this finely crafted and compellingly readable book, Dr. Myers sensitively and humanely communicates the stories of the families and loved ones of physicians who have died by suicide, explaining that their observations "capture the complexity, the inner conflict and the irony of self-destruction and despair in our guardians of life." He also opens a window into the guarded and protected culture of the medical profession and the resulting stigma and secrecy that stands in the way of understanding why so many doctors take their own lives.

Dr. Myers not only helps us see the factors that contribute to suicide in the medical profession but also offers practical and pioneering solutions about how to prevent even more suicides from occurring. His groundbreaking book is the first step in acknowledging that physician suicide is a growing problem that must be addressed, both for physicians as well as their families and all who care for them.

"We must keep talking about a subject that, sadly, is not going away," Dr. Myers concludes. *Why Physicians Die by Suicide* is an invaluable resource that is much needed, much welcomed, and much appreciated.

Carla Fine, author of *No Time to Say Goodbye:*
Surviving the Suicide of a Loved One

Introduction

"A good friend told me about her death. We didn't know right away that it was suicide. It was horrible to hear the truth. It came out that she had been struggling. Why is there so much stigma? Why is there that message of 'don't show any weakness' in the everyday world of medicine?"

The words of Pam Swift, MD, author of *Doctor's Orders: One Physician's Journey Back to Self.* I spoke to her by telephone on September 18, 2015 about the loss of a doctor colleague to suicide.[1]

In the fall of 1962, I was a nineteen-year-old first year medical student and had gone home to Chatham, Ontario for the weekend to celebrate Thanksgiving with my parents. I was looking forward to getting back to classes and the apartment I shared with three other medical students, Bill, Graham and Henry.

I remember parking my car in front of the duplex and saw our normally ebullient landlady standing at the front entrance. She looked tense and distraught as she asked me to come into her apartment for a few minutes. She told me to sit down and then she said, "I have some very sad news. It's about Bill. Bill's parents called a couple of hours ago. They said he won't be coming back to medical school. He died over the weekend. They said it was suicide."

I felt like I had been kicked in the stomach. Bill had been found dead in his car, parked on a lonely stretch of beach on Lake Huron, with a hose running from the exhaust pipe into the interior. Like almost all survivors, I didn't see it coming. My mind went into overdrive. What did he mean on Wednesday night – the last I saw him alive – when he said "See you after the weekend?" Was there some cryptic message? Was he depressed, desperate? Did his face look different or his voice sound tentative?

I went into our apartment and just kind of wandered a bit in a daze. Kind of stunned. Henry, a fourth year medical student, was in Africa on a month long elective in tropical medicine. I talked for a while with Graham, also a senior student, but it was really awkward. He had to study for an exam so he went to his room and closed the door. I did get some sleep but not much.

The next morning, I asked our biochemistry professor if I could make a brief announcement before he began. I will never forget standing in front of my classmates and telling them that Bill had died by suicide over the weekend. I remember my wobbly knees and quivering voice, stuttering over the word "suicide." I especially recall my classmates' frozen and pale faces. I told them I would keep them updated as I learned more. Then I returned to my seat. The professor broke the silence and awkwardly said, "So let's return to the Krebs cycle."

But I never learned more. I did call Bill's parents to ask about the funeral arrangements, but his father, although polite, was curt and said that it was private. There was no information from the Dean's office, no announcement. No one spoke to our class. We did not send flowers or a card to the family. It was as if Bill had never existed. I look back now and think it would have been very different if he were killed in a car accident.

I buried myself in my studies, which is easy enough to do in medical school, where the work load and the pressure to do well are immense. But I wasn't entirely successful in blocking out Bill's death – or, more important, his life. There were reminders around the apartment. Although his parents came and packed up all his clothes and other personal effects, they left his books. They had no need for them. I was too young to realize the symbolism in this gift. That a part of Bill could live on and remain connected to me or the medical school.

It was so sad to walk by his empty room every day after class. I was comforted by the brief moments when I saw him, albeit fleetingly, at his desk studying. I knew he was dead but this vision didn't alarm me. Only later, when I studied psychiatry, and bereavement in particular, did I learn that seeing the image of a familiar one for weeks or months after their death is quite normal. The three of us decided not to advertise for another roommate and just absorb the cost. Henry and I spoke about Bill a couple of times. Graham never mentioned him again. At the end of the academic year, we gave up the apartment. They both graduated and headed away to do their internships. I started a summer research project and moved into a fraternity house on campus.

In 2015, more than 44,000 Americans killed themselves.[2] This means that in the United States one person dies by suicide every twelve minutes. It is the tenth most common cause of death in the country, and despite much fine research and improved prevention initiatives and treatment methods, the suicide rate has been climbing steadily over the past fifteen years. Perhaps equally distressing, more than one million people attempt suicide each year – that equates to one attempt every thirty-five seconds. In a country with declining mortality, death by suicide has become a public health imperative.

It is generally believed that somewhere between 85 and 90 percent of individuals who kill themselves are suffering from a psychiatric illness at the time of their death. The most common diagnoses are depression, alcoholism and other substance use disorders, posttraumatic stress disorder, bipolar illness, psychotic disorders (including schizophrenia), painful or chronic medical disorders, and various types of personality problems. Some individuals who die by suicide are fighting a number of these illnesses simultaneously. What is dangerous – and so heart breaking – is that so many sufferers are either not receiving proper treatment or that the treatment is simply not working. The psychological pain becomes unbearable, the person feels increasingly hopeless, a one-track mind eclipses rational thought, and self-extinction appears to be the only way out.

So how do doctors fit into this picture? The American Foundation for Suicide Prevention estimates that 300-400 physicians die by suicide each year – the equivalent of one a day, every day of the week. And the actual number is believed to be even higher, because in some cases the manner of death may be ruled natural or by accident (as, for example, a single motor vehicle death). And in some rare cases a coroner or physician may cover up the true cause when filling out a death certificate for a fellow physician or colleague.

Male physicians kill themselves at a slightly higher rate than men in the general population. Women physicians die by suicide at a rate of 2 to3 times that of women in the general population. And, unlike almost all other population groups, in which men die by suicide about four times more frequently than women, physicians have a suicide rate that is very similar for women and men.

To some degree, the higher than average rate for women physicians, could be explained by some of the same gender inequalities that we see in the general population. Although women account for approximately half of all medical students and residents today, there remain vestiges of institutional sexism in our medical centers. Sexual harassment and mistreatment in medical colleges and hospitals are much less frequent than in the past but not wholly eradicated. Salaries for the same work are not always equal. Even in the most egalitarian of medical marriages, women physicians remain, for the most part, the CEOs of the home. Constantly striving for balance, they may be more stressed than their husbands. Medicine is no longer a man's profession, but it can be a tough job.

We know that women in medicine tend to "give more" to their patients, which translates to spending more time with them and addressing their psychosocial issues more than men in medicine usually do. It is possible that these particular qualities, while obviously good for their patients, do not necessarily serve women well when coping with the day-to-day realities of how contemporary medicine works. We need to do more research into the psychological treatment of women physicians when they become symptomatic. What are their unique conflicts, needs and vulnerabilities, and the most effective approaches to addressing them?

There is no one factor that drives someone to kill himself. It takes a combination of pressures and losses including biological, psychological, cultural, economic, legal, spiritual and more, most, if not all of which apply to suicidal people in general, but also many that are unique to physicians.

That said, it is important to understand that the vast majority of doctors are fit and resilient. Even most of those who do have psychiatric illnesses, addictions to drugs or alcohol, or to behaviors such as gambling or sex, do not kill themselves. But even one death by suicide is too many. Just ask any family who has lost a dear loved one to suicide.

For too long, at least until 1970, medical students and physicians who killed themselves were considered outliers, misfits or, even worse, individuals whose deaths sullied the profession and who should never have been admitted into the medical profession in the first place.

Thankfully, that kind of thinking is no longer the norm. In mid-August of 2014, the New York City academic medical community was rocked by the devastating news of two young interns who killed themselves within a few days of each other. There was an immediate notice and alert composed by the President and CEO of the medical institution and disseminated to all training programs in the city. It was a call to arms for all training directors and deans of postgraduate medical education to enhance their outreach to residents and fellows. In response to the tragedy, a beautifully crafted, heartfelt op ed piece by Dr. Pranay Sinha, an intern at Yale, was published in *The New York Times* entitled "Why Do Doctors Commit Suicide?".[3] He called for a change in the culture of medicine, one that would encourage residents to openly share their vulnerabilities and forge connections with each other. I responded with a letter-to-the-editor urging medical faculty and the supervisors and mentors of our trainees to follow suit.[4]

Then, in September, *Slate* published a passionate and powerful article entitled "Tyranny of Perfection" by Dr. Danielle Ofri, internist at Bellevue Hospital and Associate Professor of Medicine at New York University. She pulled no punches ("the raw pain in the medical community is palpable") and examined how tough it is in the everyday world of medicine to set appropriate standards of training and care yet guard against overshooting and missing the early signs of strain, depression, substance use and suicidality in our residents and colleagues.[5]

Both Dr. Sinha's op ed piece and Dr. Ofri's *Slate* article received hundreds of comments, and not just from those in the health professions. A national conversation is underway. People care about the wellbeing of doctors and are horrified by the unhealthy situations that are, at least in part, contributing to the self-inflicted deaths of their healers. What these responses indicate is that people in general are able to see beyond the trappings of status, privilege, and a comfortable life style to the fatigue, heartache, loneliness, and despair of doctors who are at risk.

Both as a practicing clinician treating physicians and their families and as an academician, I have spent my entire career studying the tragedy and enigma of suicide among doctors. Despite substantial research into the personal and workplace stressors, personality traits, psychological vulnerabilities, and psychiatric illnesses among doctors, the published literature is short on information gleaned from those who know physicians best – their family members, medical colleagues, and intimate friends, their teachers and students, as well as those who have lost their physicians to suicide. I have long believed that these are exactly the people who hold information that is key to our quest to make sense of why some doctors make such a desperate decision about their life.

For more than two years I have been talking with those who are willing to share their story and understanding of the physician loved one, colleague/friend, or treating doctor whom they've lost. In the pages that follow, you will hear their voices, and I will share what I have learned from them, as well as from another, equally significant population--physicians (including some of my own patients) who have attempted suicide and did not die. They are able to provide unique and invaluable information about the ideas and emotions that led to their decision to kill themselves as well as the ways in which their near-death experience and second chance at living have fundamentally changed them.

Although suicide has been with us since the beginning of time, it remains a very taboo subject in our society. Many people do not want to know about it and when they do they want to push it way, to forget about it, trying hard not to remember. I am only too aware of this. I sense it when I face the resistance to my research or the derision I get from a few of my colleagues about "being obsessed with suicide". We write about very different subjects but I feel great kinship with the late Elie Wiesel. In accepting the Nobel Peace Prize in 1986, he said, "...I have tried to keep memory alive...I have tried to fight those who would forget. Because, if we forget, we are guilty, we are accomplices."

As painful as suicide is, we must remember our brothers and sisters in medicine who could not go on, whose lives were so tragically interrupted. Many of the people with whom I spoke in preparation for writing this book have told me that they were sharing their stories because they didn't want their loved one to have died in vain, and they hoped what they had to say would in some way contribute to saving the life of another despairing physician. In the words of Dr. Edwin Shneidman who was a Professor of Psychology at UCLA, esteemed researcher, prolific author and giant in the study of suicide: "Postvention is prevention for the next generation."

PART ONE

UNDERSTANDING PHYSICIANS AND THEIR WORLD

CHAPTER 1

CHARACTERISTICS OF PHYSICIANS: STRENGTHS AND VULNERABILITIES

When word got around Centerville that Dr. James had died by suicide, the entire community was in a state of disbelief. As a third-generation physician in a small Midwestern town, he was known and well loved by every one of its 10,000 citizens. He was not only the primary care doctor to many of them; he was also the mayor. Everyone loved Dr. James. He was indefatigable, committed to his patients and their families, generous to a fault and a dedicated husband and father. It meant a lot to these proud folks that he had not been lured to the bright lights and big bucks of the nearby metropolis. But their shock and incredulity quickly gave way to a profound and deep sorrow that was gut-wrenching for many and paralyzing for others. In his medical office, the town hall, cafes, parks and homes, people cried openly and without shame. Centerville shut down for the afternoon of his funeral as mourners filled the church.

This is a composite story of several anecdotes shared with me by my patients and colleagues

According to the Federation of State Physician Health Programs, in 2014 there were 916,264 licensed physicians in the United States. They vary tremendously in appearance, temperament, spirituality and political persuasion as well as in age, gender, race, ethnicity, marital status, sexual orientation and gender identity. They may be MDs, osteopaths, US- or foreign-trained. To my knowledge, no descriptive studies of suicidal doctors or doctors who have succumbed to suicide have confirmed any single characteristic or group of variables that should raise red flags and help us in prevention. There are known risk factors, but they are not necessarily predictive of suicide. At the end of the day, suicide can happen to anyone. The notion that anyone is immune is simply an illusion.

WHAT ABOUT PERSONALITY CHARACTERISTICS?

Dr. Jonathan Drummond-Webb was a rising star in the field of pediatric heart surgery. Born in Johannesburg, South Africa, he came to the United States in 1995 to do a surgical fellowship. In 1997 he did a second fellowship at the prestigious Cleveland Clinic. While there, he became the surgical director of pediatric cardiac and lung transplantation. Finally, in 2001 he was named chief of pediatric and congenital cardiac surgery at the Arkansas Children's Hospital in Little Rock, Arkansas. There he was the first endowed chair in pediatric and congenital cardiac surgery. Three years after arriving, on the day after Christmas, he killed himself.

> *In the midst of the shock and grief, Dr. Jonathan R. Bates, President and CEO of Arkansas Children's Hospital, made the following observation: "Some would say they saved 98 out of 100; Dr. Drummond-Webb said, 'I lost two out of 100.'" (Associated Press 2004)*[6]

Even though the act of suicide is a complex phenomenon involving some convergence of genes, psychology, and psychosocial stressors, we can often learn something fundamental about the psychology of physicians by studying the lives of those with the most tragic outcomes.

Chapter 1: Characteristics of Physicians: Strengths and Vulnerabilities

Dr. Bates's observations about Dr. Drummond-Webb, for example, resonate with most physicians to some degree. He paints a portrait of a man who was haunted by his failures. His many successful accomplishments somehow did not compensate for his occasional unsuccessful attempts to save a child in distress. We do not, of course, know all of the factors that contributed to Dr. Drummond-Webb's suicide. It was reported that his friends believed he suffered from a sudden bout of depression. Nevertheless, the perfectionism and self-recrimination described by Dr. Bates are traits common to most physicians and can torment even those who do not become suicidal.

The Tyranny of Perfectionism

In terms of the various characteristics that coalesce in defining physicians, perfectionism is one that stands out as a known risk factor for suicide.[7] Perfectionism can be a double-edged sword. In terms of the positive aspects that apply to physicians, many are ambitious and driven from a very young age to get good grades and succeed at whatever other accomplishments will help to ensure that they get into medical school. They thrive on the high standards of excellence and precision required by their chosen profession, and enjoy the satisfaction that accrues to hard work, focus, and academic rigor. Given the rapidly changing scientific discoveries in medicine and its day-to-day practice, most doctors need some degree of perfectionism to adapt and stay at the top of their game.

The widow of one physician who killed himself several years ago put it this way:

My husband was a relentless perfectionist. I adored him. When he committed suicide, I thought that no one would ever love me the way Sam loved me. He took pills and Scotch. The pills were self-prescribed; there was a bill from the pharmacy after he died. He did it in his office. His father also died by suicide, but the family covered it up. They said it was cancer. He was a doctor too. Sam had too much compassion and not enough steel. He was brilliant. I respected his intelligence. He was so classy. People took advantage of him. He was repressed. I represented freedom to him. He couldn't live in the real world. Problems with his kids from an earlier marriage weighed on him. He got depressed and refused to see a psychiatrist; he just withdrew into a dream world. Then he was gone.

In this man's case, one can speculate that his perfectionism contributed to his depression, an illness that he may have been vulnerable to, and in part, inherited from his father. The negative aspects of perfectionism are troublesome. According to the Center for Clinical Interventions,[8] perfectionism has three key components:

1. The relentless striving for extremely high standards

2. Judging your self-worth based largely on your ability to strive for and achieve such unrelenting standards

3. Experiencing negative consequences of setting such demanding standards, yet continuing to go for them despite the huge cost to you

Physicians who are on the extreme end of the perfectionism continuum push themselves over and over again to improve and do better. They are extremely hard on themselves if they make a mistake or don't excel in virtually everything they do. They don't relax easily and feel guilty if they lie in a hammock reading a trashy novel or play a video game instead of reading the current issue of the *New England Journal of Medicine*. Inwardly they are also very competitive with their peers but rarely acknowledge this to their loved ones, medical colleagues, or friends. Some are envious of those who win prizes, awards or honors for their medical achievements. The rewards given to others can make them feel inferior. They may be jealous of doctors in their branch of medicine who make the Best Doctors in America list (although they mock its reliability) or of those who have bigger homes in more prestigious neighborhoods and those who take more exotic family vacations.

This is an approach to life that can put a terrible strain on marriage.[9]

> *Dr. C ("Dr. Control" as his wife called him), an infectious disease specialist and academic, and his wife, a homemaker and community volunteer, were referred to me by a psychiatrist colleague who was treating Mrs. C for depression. In psychotherapy, Mrs. C complained bitterly about her husband's behavior toward her at home – grilling and "put downs" – all of which affected her self-confidence and didn't help her mood.*

> *Our initial visit began with a bang. Detained at the hospital with a suicidal patient, I was five minutes late. I apologized. Dr. C looked at his watch and asked, "Will you be making up the time today or at the next visit, if there is one?" I apologized again and invited them to talk about their concerns. Mrs. C seemed embarrassed and nervous; her speech was faltering and digressive. Impatient to get on with it, Dr. C interrupted with "Let me explain. We're here because my wife and her female psychiatrist think that I'm a control freak. I don't totally disagree but I don't totally agree either. I am a very organized and exacting person – I don't suffer fools gladly. I didn't get to be a division chief at the age of thirty-five for no good reason. Meredith is different from me, aren't you dear? Quite laid back. Why do you bristle when I ask you about your*

day? Aren't you responsible for the running of the home? I just want to make sure that you're doing it properly."

I asked Mrs. C to respond. "Here's how you ask about my day, Peter," she said. You don't even say hello or hug me like you used to. You walk in the back door and start with your laundry list: 'Did you water the flowers on the front deck? Why isn't the car in the garage? I thought you were going to call someone to get that gutter fixed? Why isn't Marcus practicing his violin? Who left the light on in the basement? You didn't bake another apple pie, did you? You know that Josh can't have any; he's really getting fat. What an enabler you are. I hope you didn't forget the dry cleaning.'."

Not surprisingly, Dr. C reacted defensively and with long explanations for all his questions. He couldn't see that it was his manner that rankled. I got both of them off this subject in order to learn more about the history of their marriage and their three sons, who were teenagers at the time. At that point they both brightened up, lightened up, and found some affection for each other. The visit ended on a better note than it began.

Their subsequent individual sessions helped a lot. Mrs. C told me that her husband hated to go to bed alone. When she wanted to stay up later and held her ground, he got very angry, more demanding, and sometimes stormed out of the house. This frightened her.

I learned that Dr. C was an only child who was adored by his somewhat older parents. He was an anxious child whose books and toys had to be "just so" before he got into bed; he slept with his nightlight on until university (and beyond); he worried that his parents might divorce; he worried that he'd fail an exam and not be number one in his class; he had very few friends, and he hated sports. "I was kind of a nerd, but what the hell, look what a success I've become."

Dr. C's perfectionism acted as a cover for his anxiety, self-reproachful thinking, wobbly self-esteem, and sadness. In fact, perfectionism is one of the biggest triggers for depression, which is the price to be paid for having set the bar so high. The self-reproach of intensely perfectionistic physicians is terrible, exhausting, and defeating. In fact, it is even upsetting and painful for the mental health professional treating such individuals to listen to their relentless self-flagellating, which is a sign that the patient is very seriously ill and may be verging on psychosis. It is also one of the most dangerous components in the mindset of desperate doctors who kill themselves.

Physicians who "stand out" amongst their peers

Some physicians are multi-talented and seem to have it all. They are very bright with impressive academic pedigrees, and in addition to their medical skills, they often excel at other endeavors. They may play the piano very well; they could be great athletes, extremely popular, and have a great sense of humor. Maybe they care deeply about social justice and give of themselves to causes. They have lots of energy and always seem happy. They are ambitious and very goal-oriented. They expect to do well in medicine, and others expect that of them as well. They are, in fact, the last people you would imagine ever killing themselves.

Anthony Halperin was one of those superstars who took his own life a few short weeks before graduating from the University of Pennsylvania medical school in 2011. His older brother, Alex, wrote about him in Salon two years later:

In school, "He did everything exactly how it should be done or you fantasize it should be done," my father said. Even as he excelled, Anthony's good looks and athleticism freed him from the social death of being a smart kid in high school. "He was very handsome, [he had] a lot of girlfriends, and he was invited to do everything," my mother said. "He really was a star. You just felt better when you were around him…If you were his friend, you felt as you've elevated yourself in a way, and I think that was the draw, but he wasn't a snob. I don't think he had a great sense of humor, but he appreciated people who did. He himself was not lighthearted, he wasn't jovial and spontaneous, I don't think, but I think he liked to be around people who were.

She went on: "He was a perfectionist. Ninety-five, to him, was a failing grade. He was also very generous with his knowledge. He helped people a lot, in school…He wanted everyone to succeed."[10]

His sister, Dr. Anna Rosen, whom I interviewed for this book told me that, "Anthony didn't realize he was in such a severe depression; he didn't have the experience that I have as a psychiatrist. No one could understand why he'd be depressed. And I think that this inhibited him from getting treatment. He was gifted, he was super-smart, his work ethic was profound. I said 'Anthony, please see someone' [meaning a psychiatrist]. But he was super-averse to seeking treatment. He was too ill to think it through."

Dr. Tom Baxter was another stand-out, who died by suicide while embarking on sub-specialty training. As far as anyone knew, he had never been depressed in his life. His undergraduate degree, medical school, and residency training were all completed at prestigious academic institutions. He was hugely popular and always upbeat. He was warm and caring. Everyone loved him, including his patients.

According to his sister, "Tom was a renaissance man, gifted, touched by light, brilliant, creative, and so well-rounded. He could have done anything.

CHAPTER 1: CHARACTERISTICS OF PHYSICIANS: STRENGTHS AND VULNERABILITIES

He made people laugh. He won every award and had so many accomplishments. He worked hard and played hard. There was no evidence of darkness, of depression. He was highly sensitive. One of his mentors compared him to Van Gogh. He had a heightened sense of feeling, an intensity. There were no signs."

And, as a friend and roommate from medical school put it, "Tom was the last person I'd expect this to happen to. He was remarkable...so talented...he was a musician...and he was very funny...he had a great social life. I know now that this could happen to anyone. He helped me through a rough time when we were in medical school...it's so sad that he couldn't reach out...that I didn't get a chance to help him...I just wish he would've reached out."

WHAT ABOUT SENSITIVITY?

A number of the individuals I spoke to described their loved one as sensitive, often "very" sensitive or "more sensitive than the average doctor." These doctors, I was told, cared deeply about their patients and took criticism seriously, even perhaps more personally than they should. As an educator and program administrator for medical students and residents, I am troubled by the sad irony here. We look for sensitivity in applicants to medical school and residency, and it is frightening to think that so positive an attribute can be part of the volatile mix that leads to suicide in distressed doctors.

Susan Solovay, who lost her brother to suicide in 2015, described him this way: "He was male and female – he had soul – he was supersensitive; he was very happy in medicine; he gave so much; he was very technical too. My brother was a giver; he was amazing; he was an incredible doctor. He had had depression before, in college and in medical school. He disclosed this but he was so ashamed."

And a female doctor who asked to remain anonymous, said that the brother she lost to suicide "was a very loving person. He loved his family. He was very concerned about his patients. He struggled with depression before going to medical school. He loved to help the underserved. He really cared. He couldn't deal with conflict. His death is such a loss – to his family, to his patients, and to society."

Film maker Sally Heckel lost her father, Dr. George Heckel, to suicide in 1963. She was seventeen, her father was fifty-four. Her beautiful and powerful film, *Unspeakable,* charts his descent into depression and its profound impact on the family.[11] When I spoke with her about him, she said that he "was always interested in science, in medicine. He had a very sensitive side, an artistic element. He took things much harder than others. His depression was gradual and it kept increasing. A female friend of his said he just slowly got more and more remote. He was shy. He got quieter and quieter at home. He would sit in his chair and just stare. It was like a pall, if you walked into the room."

THE NARCISSISTS

Despite the fact that physicians are often revered and honored in our society, the vast majority of them are not narcissists. Like perfectionism, narcissism exists on a continuum. In fact, the expression "healthy narcissism" is particularly apt when describing a successful physician. This is someone who possesses enough self-regard, confidence, and ambition to feel worthy and secure in pushing forward to compete for the position or job he wants, and who bounces back and explores other options when/if that doesn't happen. Patients want their physician to be not only smart and savvy but confident when diagnosing their symptoms and recommending the best treatment options. When I once asked a patient of mine how she felt about her new and very popular breast surgeon, her reply was, "She's pretty full of herself but what the hell, she's got a great reputation and I'm sure she's worked hard to get it. I trust her with my life. But that's not the full story. She's also very compassionate and I like that." This is what I would call healthy narcissism.

Problematic narcissism can, however, be a risk factor for suicide, because what may appear as rock solid self-regard is actually build on an extremely fragile base. Although the doctor may seem to have it all – a successful practice or corporate/academic title, money, good looks, health, seemingly perfect family and so on – this is not the way he feels inside. In fact, pathologically narcissistic doctors do not have the solid core of basic strength and self-esteem that would see them through tough times. Instead, they crumble and implode. This is a life-long pattern, probably resulting from some combination of genetics and complicated parenting. They require constant reassurance and stroking to feel good about themselves. Therefore, these so-called "prominent" physicians can crash into a suicidal state when suffering too many simultaneous losses or assaults, or a trauma that is especially shameful, such as being fired from a world class medical facility, being charged with Medicaid fraud or being accused of sexual indiscretions with patients.

You might wonder "Wouldn't these stressors be enough to push any doctor over the edge?" Yes and no. Yes, these are crushing accusations, but most physicians are surprisingly adaptive in working closely with their defense attorneys and willingly seeking professional mental health care for the state they're in. Narcissistic individuals, however, often deny that they're severely affected by these blows or do not recognize how tattered they've become. They have trouble seeing how their air of entitlement gets them into trouble with others or how they are blind to the consequences of their unprofessional, unethical or illegal behavior. And if they are disdainful of or contemptuous of mental health professionals, they don't engage or commit to working at getting better. They sabotage potentially life-saving care.

The Wounded Healer

The term "wounded healer" was first coined by Swiss psychiatrist and psychoanalyst Carl Jung, who saw its origins in Greek mythology. Chiron was physically wounded, and by overcoming the pain of his own wounds, he became the compassionate teacher of healing. The expression is used today to include people in the helping professions – physicians, nurses, psychologists, social workers, and other counselors and the clergy – who are drawn to their work at least in part because of their own wounds, which, in turn, help them to recognize, empathize with, understand, and heal the wounds of their patients and clients. The list of stressors that are deemed wounding or traumatic is huge: abuse, divorce, poverty, immigration, hunger, mental illness, physical injury, cancer, hospitalization, bigotry, and more. In short, the human condition. Very few medical students come from privileged families and TV-drama-perfect parents.

Herein lies the paradox: Some of the most accomplished and successful physicians with less than ideal ancestry cope magnificently with their work and with navigating family issues. They do not miss a beat when their younger sibling is incarcerated for drug dealing, their bipolar father is picked up by the police for talking gibberish on a New York subway platform, or their mother is embarking on her fourth divorce. However, they do pay a price, and that is neglecting themselves.

Since childhood they have been serving others – initially family members and now both their patients and their families. As a result, their physical and mental health may suffer. They often do not eat properly, exercise, nurture avocations, or take time for self-reflection. They may deal with their anxiety, worry, or despondency by working even harder, drinking, smoking, or using other addictive drugs. They rarely have a personal physician to whom they can turn for medical supervision of their health, advice, and support through tough times. Isolation plus unhealthy habits make for a toxic mix

CHAPTER 1: CHARACTERISTICS OF PHYSICIANS: STRENGTHS AND VULNERABILITIES

that, over time, can lead to suicidal despair and recklessness. Here is a disguised example from my own practice.

"I'm broken, Dr. Myers" said Dr. A, a general internist and my new patient, in a voice barely above a whisper. I asked him to explain and leaned forward to hear him better. "It's physical and it's mental. I'm forty-six years old by the calendar, but my soul is eighty. I look in the mirror and I see sagging defeat. My joints are wrong; they feel out of alignment; they're sore and painful and stiff. I've thought of a cane but that's too conspicuous because…I'm a shy man. The systems are slowed — circulatory, respiratory, digestive, and urinary — but thyroid function is normal. It's the brain and the mind that prompt this visit. Are they the same? I make a distinction. My brain is sluggish, it's not working right. Like I've had an infarct, a stroke without peripheral signs. Or that I'm hypoxic or have cerebral edema. Something is wrong, out of order. All I can do is guess. I've lost thoughts, words, sentences — gone I don't know where. The mind is worrying me. What mind? The mind is lost, devoid of spirit. It's like a flat tire, deflated, of no use any more. Can't be counted on. My brain thinks that my mind should be terrified about this. How I wish for that, for some emotion. But that's gone too, kaput. Maybe that's a big enough chief complaint. Forgive me for talking so much. Do you think you can help? I think I need more than glue."

When I inquired about suicidal thinking he replied in a monotone, "Of course I've had a lot of thoughts of wanting to die and of killing myself, but I'm not dangerous to myself. I'm too sick to do it. My brain can't get it together. I would botch it."

I was still a young psychiatrist at the time, and frightened by my patient's symptoms and suffering. I wanted to make the right diagnosis – fast – and get him treated and well again. Thankfully, he did very well with psychiatric hospitalization, a course of electroconvulsive therapy, medication, and supportive psychotherapy over a two year period. I include his story here because he is a classic example of the wounded healer:

- He had been physically and emotionally abused as a boy by a sadistic father

- He had to learn English from scratch when the family emigrated from India when he was ten years old

- He was teased and bullied as an ethnic minority pupil in his "vanilla" community

- He worked tirelessly at school and at jobs to help support the family

- He married during medical school and started a family immediately

- After graduating, he worked almost seven days a week as a primary care doctor in their small rural community

- He rarely took time off or had a vacation

- He and his wife lived together but were quite estranged and he had slept in the basement for years

- He was drinking significantly when he became my patient and argued that he drank "to give me some peace."

A LETHAL TRIFECTA

Dr. Thomas Joiner, a professor of psychology at Florida State University and an eminent researcher into the causes of suicide, believes that an individual is at high risk for suicide if three conditions are met simultaneously.[12] First, the individual feels that he or she is a burden on others (perceived burdensomeness). Second, the individual no longer feels that he belongs to a valued social group (failed belongingness). And third, the individual has acquired an ability to carry out a lethal plan of self-injury (learned fearlessness). It is the last of these that is particularly worrisome in physicians.

Joiner believes that physicians are especially vulnerable to suicide because the nature of their work exposes them to the pain and injury of their patients. This would be particularly true of surgeons and emergency physicians who are exposed to patients hurt in accidents or who have tried to die by shooting or stabbing themselves, setting themselves on fire, or jumping from heights. Psychiatrists are also at increased risk because they are indirectly exposed by listening to the stories of their suicidal patients and treating those who have made attempts on their lives. This kind of secondary or indirect exposure is called vicarious trauma, and coupled with the other factors listed above could render the physician susceptible to harming him or herself.

THE FACE THEY SHOW THE WORLD

The image might be cool, handsome and "Prince Charming" – the Dr. Shepherd "McDreamy" type of Grey's Anatomy. Or self-centered, quick-tempered, yet giving – the Dr. Doug Ross type of ER. Or, for female doctors, it might be independence and the ability to practice frontier medicine and fall in love like Dr. Quinn, Medicine Woman, or young, smart, and sassy, like the women on ER. Whatever the physician's image, however, professionalism is always at its core.

Professionalism requires that the practitioner strive for excellence in the following areas:

- **Altruism**: A physician is obligated to attend to the best interest of patients, rather than self-interest.

- **Accountability**: Physicians are accountable to their patients, to society on issues of public health, and to their profession.

- **Excellence**: Physicians are obligated to make a commitment to life-long learning.

- **Duty**: A physician should be available and responsive when "on call," accepting a commitment to service within the profession and the community.

- **Honor and integrity**: Physicians should be committed to being fair, truthful and straightforward in their interactions with patients and the profession.

- **Respect for others**: A physician should demonstrate respect for patients and their families, other physicians and team members, medical students, residents and fellows. [13]

All of which should be modeled by mentors and teachers and become part of the attitudes, behaviors, and skills integral to patient care.

As a psychiatrist who treats ailing physicians I know how difficult it is for doctors to uphold the demands of their professional persona. The problem is that, too often, when they are under stress professionally and personally, these same doctors may not realize how much their professionalism has become diminished and tarnished. They may be oblivious, but their medical colleagues, students, superiors, and patients are not. In many instances, however, it is only when a complaint is made to someone in authority that the problem is addressed, a thorough independent assessment is recommended and a treatment plan is generated.

There is an old adage in medicine that says, "the last thing to go is your work." What this means is that physicians whose personal lives are falling

CHAPTER 1: CHARACTERISTICS OF PHYSICIANS: STRENGTHS AND VULNERABILITIES

apart or who drink a lot or who are suffering from depression seem to continue working as if nothing is wrong. They are never late for the operating room, they see dozens of patients each day in their clinic, they respond immediately to their pager or cell phone and they seem on top of their game. I used to think that the physician was so dedicated to medicine that he or she didn't really care if the rest of his/her life was a shambles. In other words, medicine and only medicine defined the doctor. But I know now that this is really a myth. The physician's work is indeed affected. There are subtle (and not so subtle) changes in precision and safety. Errors of omission and commission are occurring but are not immediately recognized or recorded by others. Or sometimes coworkers and staff enable dysfunction by covering up for the person, making excuses and taking up the slack. In the end, it is often the patients who, in hindsight, realize that their doctor seemed rushed, preoccupied, forgetful, was not listening or caring as he used to, and might also have been less well groomed.

As one such doctor's daughter described him to me:

> My father was a psychiatrist. He was in his early forties when he died. I was eleven. It was a scary and confusing time. He was a wonderful man, really smart and the life of the party. He worked a lot, in private practice. I'm still dealing with his death. I've been in one-on-one therapy off and on and now I go to group therapy. He had bipolar, called manic depressive illness then. I remember him being sick a lot, depressed. He'd stay in his room all weekend. I also remember him being manic. It could be scary; he would drive really fast. He had an affair about a year before he died. I also think he had an addiction problem and this affected his functioning, his judgment. After he died, I learned that a couple of families sued him because of malpractice allegations. His psychiatrist had moved away, so he was treating himself. I was told at first that he accidentally overdosed on

medication. Then I was told he died of a disease. I've concluded after many years that it was suicide. My mother has only been able to use the word "suicide" in the past year or two.

The words of the loved ones of doctors who have taken their own lives are treasures because they capture the complexity, the inner conflict and the irony of self-destruction and despair in our guardians of life. Ultimately, they shine much needed light on the darkness and confusion of suicide.

Chapter 2

The Culture of Medicine

Suicide is always a tragedy; a physician's suicide is a travesty.

from *"Silence is the Enemy for Doctors Who Have Depression"* by Aaron E Carroll, MD, New York Times January 11, 2016[14]

The culture of medicine is defined by its values, customs, norms, expectations and limitations. There are expectations that dictate one's thinking, planning, behavior, and emotions. When the physician feels that he is living up to these expectations and doing his work well, he can derive satisfaction from that. But even the best medicine has limitations, and all doctors must learn to live with that unalterable fact.

We have seen tremendous scientific advances in discovering the causes of diseases, cures and improved treatment, safety, reduced error, technological advances in surgery, and more targeted medications in oncology and psychiatry. These are exciting and joyful experiences in the daily lives of practicing doctors. But there are also many challenges, including increased documentation, learning about Electronic Health Records (EHRs), keeping up with the latest innovations, maintaining certification and licensing, the demands of patients, threats of lawsuits, business costs and more, that create unavoidable stress.

Primary care physicians juggle the problems and needs of several patients every day. Trauma surgeons perform life-saving operations over long hours in the course of their work day. Anesthesiologists alternate between periods of high alertness and restless tedium. Psychiatrists absorb the moods, complex thoughts, abuse histories, and personalities of their patients hour after hour. Emergency physicians rush from patients with crushing chest pain to those who are high on drugs and alcohol. Oncologists spend countless hours breaking bad news while trying not to be grim and always hopeful. And so it goes for all branches of medicine. But the common denominator for all physicians is that as much as medical work is incredibly rewarding it is also challenging and tiring. For many doctors that means there is not enough time for self-care, exercise, proper nutrition, or socializing with friends outside of medicine.

Our medical journals, medical news websites and other forms of social media are filled with articles on burnout among medical students and physicians. Researchers are finding that the rates are much higher in the field of medicine (and training programs) than in all other professions and graduate programs. The most common symptoms are demoralization, loss of interest and excitement in work, diminished compassion, and a kind of fatigue that is different from feeling tired after a day of hard work and is barely relieved by days off or vacation. Burnout is an erosion of the soul, a lack of direction, an inability to take charge of one's work or one's life.

Many, if not most physicians accept the fact that medicine is not a nine to five job, that there is no set "quitting time," that they will work at least some weekends, that they will be called to the hospital in the evening or after midnight, and that much of their craft is unpredictable. They also know that lifelong learning goes with the territory and that they will always be students.

The majority do manage to balance these demands with taking time for themselves and their families, eating well (at least most of the time) and exercising regularly. But there are also those who give too much to medicine, and they are the ones who are sitting ducks for burnout and its worst-case corollary, suicide. What makes their suicide even more tragic and ironic is that, in the majority of cases, they have been killed by their work, lost their lives in the line of duty. When I have treated physicians who came to me for help, what they all seem to have in common is their bitterness and powerless rage. They are furious that they have worked so hard, given so much to others, put their own needs on the back burner, and instead of receiving thanks or appreciation, or even commiseration, they find themselves miserable and often shunned by their colleagues.

Dr. Stone, a fifty-six-year-old internist, came to see me within days of being named in a lawsuit. The patient was a woman he had treated for many years, someone whom he thought was happy with her medical care. "I'm here because last weekend I decided I have two choices," he told me, "to shoot myself and get it over with or to see a psychiatrist. I'm just kidding doc," he quickly added. "Don't take me seriously, I'm not going to kill myself. You don't need to lock me up.." But I did take him seriously. He wasn't suicidal (nor did he own a firearm) but he was certainly very unhappy, defeated, and sad. And he was very angry and bitter. "I've given my whole fucking life to medicine and what have I got outta the deal?" He was tired from decades of twelve-hour days Monday through Friday and half days on Saturday. An athlete in college and medical school, he had let his nutrition and fitness fly out the window over the years. He was grossly overweight and out of shape, and that, too, preyed on him. In fact, he even brought in his graduation photo to illustrate his point. His voice broke as he gazed at the picture: "I don't even recognize that handsome, cool ass dude." I sat quietly and listened to his sobs. And I continued to listen and listen for many visits until he began to feel better and reclaim his life.

All physicians are humbled by the patients they cannot help, the diseases with negative prognoses, the inability to spend as much time as they would like with their patients, and the shortage of doctors in many smaller and remote communities.

Very often, even the most skilled and dedicated doctor feels that he can't do it all, that she is continually falling short of her own expectations for herself. And if he doesn't share these feelings with his colleagues, he may then become anxious and worried that he is flawed or deviant, and that may be the beginning of the end. Fortunately, most doctors do not work completely independently or in isolation. They have the input of their colleagues, who are also struggling to abide by all the rules and expectations, or are getting behind, or have developed wholesome shortcuts that work without compromising professional integrity or patient safety. In today's high tech medical world, including telemedicine in its various forms, even physicians who do work in relative geographical isolation are in virtual contact with peers all over the world, and that can be very comforting. Unfortunately, not all physicians who feel they are failing or falling behind are willing or able to share. And those who fall from grace – because of a malpractice lawsuit as one example - can plummet hard and fast.

MEDICINE AS AN EXCLUSIVE CLUB

Putting the initials MD after one's name is a privilege afforded a relatively few among us, those who have been admitted to an extremely exclusive club. Even the most self-assured medical student or physician would never say that getting into the club was a cakewalk. Therefore, something has to go very wrong in that journey from the joy of getting into medical school to despair and self-annihilation down the road.

The expression "the bigger they are the harder they fall" is one way of understanding how physicians feel when they become ill. Instead of ministering to others, they are the ones who need treatment. Becoming a patient is a process that many physicians do not navigate easily. To many it seems like a loss of status, as if they were no longer worthy of the title "doctor" and had, in effect, been kicked out of the club. Their definition of the requirements for membership is rigid and exclusive: Only the able bodied – and able-minded –are welcome. Some also worry that even if they sought help, help that indeed was private and confidential, that that could be grounds for being thrown out of the club. And this anxiety is not unwarranted in those states that ask outdated (or unethical or illegal) questions on medical licensing applications or hospital credentialing forms. Questions like "Have you ever been treated for alcoholism, drug addiction or any kind of psychiatric disorder?" can send shudders down your spine!

We know that shame is often one of the many emotions overwhelming those who make that fateful decision to kill themselves, and I wonder whether doctors who take their own lives believe that they deserve to die because their illness and inability to practice medicine are bringing dishonor to the profession as a whole. Of course this kind of thinking is irrational, but from the beginning of the 20th century until roughly 1970, doctors who killed themselves were considered misfits (as I mentioned earlier) who never should have been admitted to the club in the first place. To incorporate cultural anachronisms into one's thinking and self-regard is not that big a stretch.

What follows is a conversation I had with a patient, a surgeon, about an hour after she began to wake up from a near-fatal suicide attempt by overdose:

- Me: "Do you know where you are?"

- She: "Yes, I'm in an ICU somewhere."

- Me: "Correct. Do you know what happened?"

- She: "I sure do. I took too many pills. I wanted to die. I mean...I want to die."

- Me: "I'm glad you didn't. I'm happy you survived."

- She: "You are? I'm so embarrassed. I feel ashamed of myself."

- Me: "Don't be. You're in a good place here. Nobody is judging you. The staff here just wants you to get better."

- She: "But I really blew it. What kind of surgeon can't even kill herself properly?"

- Me: (taking a risk and attempting some humor) "I didn't realize that knowing how to kill yourself was a requirement of the American Board of Surgery".

- She: (smiling slightly) "Good one, doc."

- Me: "Get a bit more rest. Then you and I have got some work to do. Your depression is still there and it's got to be treated. We'll keep you safe here until you're feeling better."

Fortunately, this doctor lived. But I am still struck by her having linked her "failed" suicide attempt with her competence as a doctor. To her way of thinking, if she were a good doctor and really deserved to be in the club of medicine, she wouldn't have survived; she would have "successfully" killed herself.

MARGINALIZATION IN MEDICINE

Sometimes even those who have gained nominal acceptance to the club feel pushed to the side, trivialized, disenfranchised and alienated. Some would add that they feel discriminated against.

The National Medical Association was founded by black physicians in 1895, a time when the majority of African Americans were disenfranchised and membership in America's professional organizations, including the American Medical Association (AMA), was restricted to whites only – a situation that continued until the civil rights legislation of the 1960s.

Although the first female graduate of a medical school was Dr. Elizabeth Blackwell in 1849, one hundred years later, in 1949, only 5.5 percent of entering medical students were women. This percentage increased during the second wave of feminism in the 1970s, and the number of women entering medical school is now roughly equal to men.

Applicants with visible disabilities were not really accepted into medical school until the 1970s. Gay and lesbian students mostly remained in the closet until the 1990s. And stellar graduates of foreign medical schools even today will not be considered for some residency programs unless they have a green card, which gives them permanent residency status.

We've come a long way over the past couple of generations, but members of minority groups – racial, ethnic, religious, sexual orientation, and gender –still describe subtle and not-so-subtle forms of discrimination and alienation. Micro-inequities exist. These are messages that physicians pick up in the medical workplace, especially large medical centers and institutions, that may be vague or elusive or contradictory but do not make them feel very good. They feel more than unsupported. They may feel undervalued and passed over. Because the messaging is not uncommonly unconscious, these same doctors may be confused by their perceptions and not wholly trust them. It is only when they talk with others in their group who have similar experiences that they realize they are not imagining things and they are not alone.

Working in a stigmatized branch of medicine, I have been listening for years to the personal accounts of physicians who feel the marginalization of mental illness. At one level this is no different from the stigma felt by all patients with psychiatric disorders, but on another level, it is very different.

Why? Because my patients would like to believe that their fellow physicians would be more enlightened, more accepting, less judgmental, less frightened, and more embracing than they generally are. What is even more disturbing is that this sense of being different prevails even among psychiatrists who struggle with mental illness. The most charitable reason I can think of as to why some psychiatrists turn their backs on colleagues who are emotionally or mentally ill is that they, most of all, understand how painful and terrifying diseases of the mind can be, and, therefore, when a fellow psychiatrist falls ill, their suffering simply hits too close to home.

About twenty years ago I treated a physician with a severe mood disorder. Shortly after being discharged from the inpatient unit of my teaching hospital, he wrote a letter-to-the-editor of our state medical journal in which he disclosed that he had been recently hospitalized for severe suicidal depression.[15] His hospitalization was not a secret in the small community where he lived and worked. Most of his doctor colleagues, friends, and patients knew that he was in the hospital. Here are some excerpts from his piece:

> *I have been surprised and disappointed by the lack of support from my physician colleagues. The number of visits I have received, both at home and in hospital, are in single figures. Not a single card has arrived. Is the stigma of depression that severe? As someone once said, "No one brings you casseroles when you're getting ECT." Physicians (and others) with depression fight an extremely lonely battle. I have found human company to be invaluable, as I am sure others have. Please support your fellow physicians with depression, rather than leaving them in isolation.*

As I write this now, so many years later, I still remember my feelings of sadness, outrage and shame. Unfortunately his experience was far from unique. His message is very similar to what Dr. Perry Baird wrote in his diary in 1944, when he was hospitalized for manic-depressive illness: "...once one has crossed the line from the normal walks of life into a psychopathic hospital, one is separated from friends and relatives by walls thicker than stone; walls of prejudice and superstition."[16]

Unfortunately, we don't seem to be much more enlightened today.

CHANGING THE PARADIGM

Consciousness-raising and a shift in thinking are in order. What all medical educators need to know is that a lot of what we teach our students about mental illness is taken personally and in reference to their own health and function. We need to get away from an "us and them" paradigm and be more inclusive. Teaching that implies "they are the patients and we are the doctors who treat them" is narrow, impersonal, and insensitive.

Medical culture must be affirming and accepting. Physicians and the doctors of tomorrow are key players and contributors. Humility is its cornerstone and must endure. Doctors must never forget that they are human too.

As Susan Sontag wrote so eloquently in her seminal book *Illness as Metaphor*:

> *Illness is the night side of life, a more onerous citizenship. Everyone who is born holds dual citizenship, in the kingdom of the well and the kingdom of the sick.*[17]

Chapter 3

The Fight to Not Become a Patient

My dad never really stuck to the treatment you provided for him, Dr. Myers. He just hated being a patient. He felt so ashamed. I tried hard too, but even my support wasn't enough.

Words spoken to me by the medical student son of my patient, a psychiatrist, at the memorial service after his death by suicide.

Imagine what it must be like to go from being the trusted, knowledgeable caregiver to being the one who is in need of care. No one actually *likes* being a patient, of course, but resistance on the part of physicians is much greater. Many years ago I attended a meeting about alcoholism among doctors and the lecturer began with a question: "Does anyone know what the MD after a doctor's name stands for?" The answer: "Massive Denial." Translation: We cannot see, will not see, refuse to see that we are having symptoms of an illness and that we need to get some care.

Many physicians equate being a patient with being flawed and unable to function as well as one's peers. This is in part true. Anyone who is feeling unwell, whatever their occupation, may not be able to work as they do normally. But many physicians can't allow this for themselves. So they work

38

through all kinds of symptoms or changes in performance and hope that, magically, it will all go away. That magical thinking may go something like this: "If I just work hard and help my patients I will be okay because I'm doing good (translate as important) work". Religiously bent doctors might consider this "doing God's work" and convince themselves that, because their work is sacred, they themselves won't get sick.

When that kind of thinking doesn't work, and they get even more weary and deflated or increase their daily use of alcohol, their illness may become entrenched, and they become trapped in a vicious circle. "Presenteeism" is the term used to describe physicians who go to work ill. They are dedicated to their patients and/or their medical students or residents and fellows and do not want to let them down. They cannot and will not take "time out" for themselves. They cling to their medical mantle and will not relinquish it, even for a short time.

But why – especially among those who know full well that treatment can – and most often does – lead to cure?

A LITTLE KNOWLEDGE IS A DANGEROUS THING

Ignorance can be bliss but this is a luxury that's systematically denied to doctors virtually from the moment they enter medical school. By graduation they must have a working knowledge of the signs, symptoms, and treatment of diseases across the medical spectrum.

Fast forward 10 years. A surgeon is going through a nasty divorce. She knows her self-esteem has taken a hit and she begins to develop panicky feelings the night before she is scheduled to perform a routine operation. She doesn't sleep well, and each day her panic attacks seem to be getting worse.

Although it's been more than a decade since she spent four weeks doing her psychiatric clerkship, she hasn't forgotten how awkward and impotent she felt trying to help her patients with depression. Now, twelve years later, she panics and thinks she might be having a nervous breakdown. She begins to worry that she's heading for a psychiatric unit herself. She's terrified.

She wonders if she should call a friend and former classmate who is now a psychiatrist. But she doesn't. She thinks she might be over-reacting and just needs to tough it out. Don't lots of doctors go through divorces without consulting a shrink? She remembers that she has a few sleeping pills prescribed by her doctor five years ago after a miscarriage. She takes one. It works. She's now sleeping better but she's still worrying a lot. She's afraid of making a mistake in the operating room or missing something when assessing a patient before surgery. She decides to "up" her running schedule and join a spin class at the gym. It helps a bit, but she can't shake the feeling that she's not herself. She's lost almost ten pounds, and it shows when she looks in the mirror. She again considers calling her old friend but again decides against it. She's simply too embarrassed. She feels like a wimp and redoubles her efforts to "get a grip."

Unfortunately, this story is not unusual. A little medical knowledge can be a nerve-wracking and dangerous thing. Possibly for the first time in a very long time, they don't know what to do, but they are still reluctant to take the next logical step, which would be to get an opinion from a mental health expert.

TipToeing into Treatment

It is the rare physician who is willing to put him or herself unreservedly in the hands of another doctor. The problem is that they know too well that even the best and most competent medical professional sometimes makes a mistake.

When they have a medical problem, such as a lump in their breast or blood in their urine, they do their homework. Those who have faith in their primary care physician usually trust the specialists whom their doctor recommends. Others call a colleague in the field whom they rely on, or they go by word of mouth. And now with social media, they can at least learn a lot by searching the internet.

But doctors struggling with psychiatric symptoms behave differently. They hesitate and hesitate and hesitate. Eventually some will make that phone call, but many don't. And to make matters worse, their isolation only compounds the problem. They don't have the advantage of an outside perspective to act as a reality check. All they have to go by are their own fears, which can really distort their thinking and take them into dark corners.

Even though psychiatrists are medical doctors, we are still fighting the longstanding stereotype, particularly among our own colleagues in other disciplines, that we are not "real doctors." And when a physician is not feeling well, is frightened, and doesn't really trust his own judgment, it is perfectly understandable that he would be wary of putting himself into in the hands of a complete stranger whose area of expertise he doesn't quite count on to begin with. As a result, tiptoeing into treatment is often the norm.

FEAR OF MEDICALIZATION

Physicians who have a lot of reasons to not feel well – their mom died last year, their father needs a nursing home, and their son is on drugs and dropped out of school –would much prefer to be told that they're "stressed" than that they suffer from depression, which is a medical disorder. Or if they're really unhappy at work and want to retire from medicine, they prefer the label of "burnout."

But, this is not always the case. Those who are truly baffled by their symptoms may be relieved (although not necessarily happy) to have a diagnosis. Suddenly, the way they've been feeling, the way they've changed, begins to make sense, and treatment equates with hope that there is a light at the end of their dark tunnel.

However, even among those who accept the need for treatment, there may remain the lingering fear of taking psychiatric medications. It's a concern that is not without reason. In addition to the fact that some people have adverse reactions to these as well as to other types of medication, the drugs we use in psychiatry are complicated, and all of them have side-effects that can range from being a nuisance to actually disabling. Surgeons may develop a tremor of their hands or a weakened grip on surgical instruments. Some older (but very effective) medications affect one's vision, and some can cause dry mouth, which could call attention to the fact that the doctor is on medication. And finally, many medications cause weight gain, which doesn't make anyone happy.

In addition to these rational concerns, however, some doctors have psychological fears of taking medication. To them it is an acknowledgement that their illness has got the better of them. It's saying, "I can't fix this myself, I need a chemical to get better." Among those who pride themselves on their toughness and self-reliance, medications are viewed as a "cop out" or a "crutch." (Interestingly, these same doctors willingly take insulin for diabetes and do not feel that they've copped out!) And some doctors who routinely prescribe medications appropriate to their own field of medicine, irrationally argue that they prefer a more "natural" or "holistic" approach to mental illness.

At the end of the day, taking (and responding to) psychiatric medication means admitting to yourself that you do have a medical disorder that requires treatment. This is not, however, an admission that you're flawed or less than or second rate. It is simply accepting the fact that you have a biological – or even psychological – vulnerability to illness that requires treatment.

CHAPTER 3: THE FIGHT TO NOT BECOME A PATIENT

Dr. Mason came to see me in the midst of a moderately severe depressive illness. She was forty-six years old, and this was a first for her. Her mother suffered from depression most of her life, which caused Dr. Mason to worry that she too might be at risk. After much discussion over the course of two or three visits, and with the development of scary and very pressing thoughts of suicide, she finally agreed to take an antidepressant in addition to weekly psychotherapy. Within three weeks she began to feel better, and in six weeks she was her old self again. She was delighted but upset that her recovery seemed to be largely the result of taking medication.

I followed Dr. Mason for several years, but her recovery was not seamless. On at least three occasions she stopped taking her medication, although she always "fessed up" after she began to get sick again, and voluntarily put herself back on her meds. Her reasoning, as she expressed it to me, was, "I've proved to myself that I need this stuff. I don't like it. I hate being dependent on a pill. You know how independent I am."

By the time she retired and moved to another city, I was seeing her only twice a year. Our visits had a refrain. Me: "How are you doing, Dr. Mason?" She: "Fine – as long as I keep taking your damn pills." We were both able to laugh as I spared her the indignity of having to take "ownership" of the medication that indeed was lifesaving for her.

On the other hand, some doctor patients are relieved – and vindicated – when medication restores their wellbeing or helps them feel better than they've ever felt before. As one of my patients so poignantly put it: "Now that I can accept that my anxiety is really a biological disorder – and that I come by it naturally in my family with a three generational history of it – I don't feel so 'fucked up,' For years I've seen myself as a mental misfit and a real loser. I've always defined myself as peripheral to my doctor peers, marginal in lots of ways. I've even coined a self-designation: 'Gen X neurasthenic.' But now I'm rethinking those years of self-criticism. I'm almost ready to call myself 'normal,' whatever that is."

PSYCHIATRIST, PSYCHOLOGIST, OR SOCIAL WORKER – AN UNEASY CHOICE

"I finally made it a condition of our marriage that he seek professional help. After one session, Harry dismissed the first psychiatrist he saw – a widely respected expert on depression – as a pompous jerk. Next he went for several visits to a social worker…He then refused to continue treatment because the social worker was, as Harry put it, too enamored by the simplistic twelve-step recovery movement."

Carla Fine *No Time to Say Goodbye: Surviving the Suicide of a Loved One*[18]

As I mentioned earlier, physicians are far from monolithic in their opinion of whom they prefer to look after them. Some will avoid psychiatrists like the plague. In addition to the reasons I've already noted, they may also be afraid of the perceived power of psychiatrists – the right to hospitalize them against their wishes, to report them to their medical licensing board or their hospital management, to pressure them to take medications, to administer ECT (electroconvulsive therapy) – among the many ways they fear psychiatrists might strip them of their professional autonomy. Are these fears exaggerated? Of course. But physicians are aware of the potential dark side that exists in all branches of medicine – and it's scary. In addition to which, if you're not feeling well, you're often not thinking clearly or rationally, and in some cases you may have lost a secure grip on reality, leading to suspicious and paranoid thinking. As a result, some physicians feel safer with psychologists and other therapists who cannot prescribe medication.

But others dismiss non-medical therapists, like psychologists and clinical social workers. They may think (or at least state) psychiatrists have the most training in mental disorders and are, therefore, the best qualified to treat them. What they may not realize – or want to acknowledge – is that psychological approaches to anxiety disorders, depression, or substance use disorders actually scare them. They are afraid of talking about and facing psychological traumas, conflicts, and/or unpleasant emotions. They would prefer the "quick fix" provided by medication.

A third option would be collaborative treatment, aka split treatment, which involves a psychiatrist who prescribes and monitors medication while a psychologist or clinical social worker provides psychotherapy. Together they are responsible for agreeing on a diagnosis and mapping out the best treatment protocol. Split treatment has been around for a very long time but has become much more prevalent in the current health-insurance climate. Although psychiatrists are, of course, trained in psychotherapy as well as prescribing medication, their fees are generally higher than those of psychologists and clinical social workers, and most insurance plans do not pay very much for psychotherapy. Hence the split treatment option.

To offset the inconvenience of having to see two mental health professionals it is absolutely essential that they keep in regular touch with each other. If a psychiatrist changes the patient's medication or if the patient is having difficulty with side-effects or coming off meds, the psychiatrist needs to let the therapist know about this. If the stress in a patient's life is building or there is some change in the direction or form of psychotherapy, the therapist should notify the psychiatrist.

Many physician patients do not like split treatment because the whole concept is foreign to them. Here are the words of one physician:

> *"Why can't my psychiatrist prescribe for me and also provide the psychotherapy? I see them as linked. I'm depressed because I'm going*

through this horrible divorce. Why do I have to get my pills from him and get pushed out the door in fifteen minutes, and not back again for a month or six weeks? Then I go across the hall or down the street to see my therapist for forty-five minutes each week? My therapist is a good guy, don't get me wrong, but I end up repeating some stuff. And when I think I'm having side-effects, he doesn't know what the hell I'm talking about. I don't blame him. He didn't go to medical school. It's weird. I'm a urologist. If I diagnose an enlarged prostate in a man, I treat that patient. Or if she's got blood in her urine I look for a tumor and operate if I find one. I see now why psychiatrists are getting labeled as pill pushers."

I am certain that I am not the only psychiatrist who thinks this man has a good point. But what isn't captured is that this is the current reality of today's insurance coverage and how tough it is for psychiatrists who accept insurance to practice medicine the way they were trained. That said, given our history in the house of medicine and the long fight to prove that our branch of medicine is no less important than any other, all psychiatrists who treat physicians need to think about this man's words. It's unfortunate that he feels "pushed out the door in fifteen minutes". Many psychiatrists try to find a middle ground with a thirty-minute visit. This is still not ideal, but it does offer some time for both medication monitoring and supportive psychotherapy.

For all the reasons discussed above, and undoubtedly many more, physicians may refuse to get the help they must, on some level, know they need, or put off treatment far longer than they should – sadly, in some instances, until it is too late. When I treat physicians who do come for help at this late stage I am blunt with them. I use a metaphor from oncology. I tell them they've got metastases. This is to highlight how serious their condition is. But I am not grim. I tell them they can be treated and survive this but I can't do it alone. We have to work together and they need to commit to fighting demons and regaining a reason for living. I also commend them for reaching out. I want to convey that I "get them", that it's been agonizing for them to make the appointment and become my patient.

PART TWO

WHY SUICIDE?

CHAPTER 4

THE LONG HISTORY OF PHYSICIAN SUICIDE: NEGLECTED INSIGHTS AND THE IRONY OF TAKING YOUR OWN LIFE

Waiting. Feeling very happy. First time I ever felt without worry, as if I were free. My heart must be strong. It won't give way...Extraordinary. Pulse running well. Feel fine – when will it be over?...God seems to be over me – just leaving for a lovely voyage, but it is slow – first time without worry.

The above is from the journal of a British physician. Heavily in debt, he decided to poison himself. While he waited to die, he took the time to treat a number of patients.[19]

A colleague of mine in England, Dr. Alannah Tomkins, a professor of history at Keele University has researched physician suicide in the nineteenth century, specifically 1800-1890. These decades generated reports of more than 280 medical men who killed themselves, and that number is believed to be a significant underestimate. Men in their thirties were most at risk and sixty percent poisoned themselves, often with prussic acid (also called cyanide). Many did not leave notes but when they did, professional causes included financial and career anxieties, and non-professional causes were things like disappointment in love. Reporting of doctors' suicides in the lay press was typically very sympathetic and often brief. In the medical press, such as the *Lancet* or *British Medical Journal,* reporting was terse or extremely muted. Dr. Tomkins concluded "that the expectations placed on doctors by their patients were high, but that pressure from within the profession (and self-expectation) was probably higher. I speculated that the increasing professionalization of medicine meant that, from the 1860s if not earlier, doctors tended to be valorized or condemned outright, meaning that it was becoming more difficult to be both a doctor and an ordinary, flawed human being."[20]

Dr. Rupinder K. Legha picks up from there in her important paper, "A History of Physician Suicide in America."[21] She writes: "This article presents the physician suicide discourse that began with a handful of articles at the turn of the 20th century and evolved into a richer, revealing narrative over the course of the next century. Two characteristic eras emerge: the Golden Age (roughly 1900–1970) and the Modern Era (approximately 1970 onwards)." The few late 19th century articles that exist were sympathetic to physicians who killed themselves and who were seen as largely reacting adversely to stressful work conditions and unregulated hours of work. But during the Golden Age, as physicians started to be viewed as more and more "special," doctors also began to see themselves as immune to psychiatric illness so that any physician who developed a mental disorder or died by suicide was seen, an outlier at best or at worst as an aberration or deviant. This perception continued until 1970 and into the Modern Era when our understanding of physician psychology, psychiatric illnesses, suicide, and the culture of medicine evolved and became better understood. State sponsored physician health programs began to spring up and more articles on the professional and personal lives of physicians appeared.

Chapter 4: The Long History of Physician Suicide

Here is an example of a physician who took his life during the Golden Age. It captures what social forces might have preyed on this man as he fell ill and received treatment. These are memories of his daughter Phyllis Wolk:

"My father's death was a Shonda (a Yiddish word meaning 'shame'). He was hospitalized several weeks before he died. It was an attempted suicide that landed him in hospital for 2 weeks, not diabetes. His doctor covered it up, so did my mother. How sad, she must have been distraught, and had no support. The story of his diabetes became the truth. I was 4 when he died. We weren't allowed to go to the funeral. I was told 'Your father went on a trip'. This story has affected me. I have been anxious before I go on a trip all my life, it's like 'Could this happen to me when I'm away, like what happened to my father?' My father was such a perfectionist. He was a wonderful research physician, he wanted to become head of internal medicine in Cleveland – but he wasn't political and didn't get it. My father was held up to us as a god…

I have two recommendations to make: One, secrecy is so destructive. It is so beneficial and clearing to talk. Don't be afraid to talk. It's been helpful to me, all my life, I still sometimes need to talk about my father's suicide. Two, medical students need to know they can't be perfect, that they are human. More needs to be done in our medical schools, there needs to be more education on the humane side of medicine."

Ms Wolk is the daughter of Dr. Maurice H Grossberg who killed himself in 1939 at the age of 43. The cause of death was called a heart attack. His widow never really talked about it. Ms Wolk did not learn the truth of her father's death until she was 65 years old. I interviewed her by telephone March 31, 2015. Parts of her story are documented in the short film "Last Glimmer of Day."[22]

And here is a second example. This is the story of another daughter, Mary Jones, who lost her physician father toward the end of the Golden

Age. She captures the profound stigma associated with mental illness in doctors at that time and how much her mother tried to protect her from knowing the true story of her father's demise:

> *"I lost my father when I was 13. It was the same week as the Aberfan disaster in Wales (October 21, 1966). He attended medical school in Liverpool but had a breakdown afterwards. Then came the war and he served in India and Burma. He probably saw a lot there. Also his mother died while he was away and he couldn't get back. After the war, he returned to England and had another breakdown. He also had diabetes and then a heart attack when he was 51. Then he was also going in for prostate surgery in Leicestershire. It was a Friday. He didn't return, he never returned. Four months later his body was found near a railway by a tree in the countryside. My first question was 'Was it suicide?' My mother said 'No, it was a heart attack."* At the inquest there was no support from the doctors or the many cousins on the other side. My grades really dropped. My report said 'bad behavior.'*

> *I trained as a teacher. In my mid-20s, I went to see my mother and asked 'Could my father's death be suicide?' She said 'there were crushed up antidepressants in his flask but it was still a heart attack.' For 13 years, no one had spoken his name. This was a breakthrough because we talked about this again and up until her death 6 years ago.*

> *How did his death affect us? Terribly! You never get over it. I wonder 'if it never happened, would I be a different person?' His family wanted nothing to do with us. My father was a fantastic photographer and I honor him for that. I just wish it would have never happened...that he had died normally."*

Telephone interview conducted October 14, 2015

As I write this, I am reminded of my roommate, Bill, who, as I've said killed himself in 1962, before the advent of the Modern Era. Although he was still a few years from being a fully qualified physician, he had met the competitive qualifications and secured a sought-after spot in medical school. I think the unspoken belief-system applied here too, that his self-destructive end was perceived as a deviant act, a bad thing, something to be hidden and not allowed to tarnish the hallowed halls of our medical school. This may explain why no one spoke to our class about his death, why no acknowledgment was made by the administration, and why we as a class, taking a lesson from our elders, became complicit in this contagious process and did nothing to honor his memory. My heart remains heavy as I reflect on his short life, but I take some small comfort in believing that it is never too late to make some form of restitution. Much of my work has been, and will continue to be, in Bill's honor.

SUICIDE – THE "DIRTY LITTLE SECRET" OF MEDICINE

I want to introduce the notion of "dirty little secret" as embedded in the culture of medicine. As much as individuals want to put their best foot forward when working with the public, physicians are no exception to this tendency, nor is medicine as a profession. The argument, arguably, is that we want our patients to have confidence in us, the services we offer and the integrity with which we conduct our trade. I'm deliberately using business language to make my point. There is a fear that if our patients knew some of our guild secrets, they may lose confidence or go elsewhere.

I present a counterargument here. The cat is already out of the bag. Stories about doctors killing themselves are featured in the general media, although fortunately due to ethical guidelines around suicide reporting in general, these reports are no longer sensationalized. But with today's social media wiring, physician suicide articles in professional journals and clinical blogs go viral very quickly. To try to suppress the reality of what is happening in the house of medicine is silly and self-defeating.

Here are some examples from the lay press that I've collected from the internet over the past few years:

"Depression led to Treuddyn doctor's suicide."

"Details of prominent doctor's murder-suicide revealed."

"Truro hospital doctor's suicide after devastating HIV diagnosis."

"Prominent Chicago heart surgeon, Dr. Hani Hennein, commits suicide after critically wounding estranged wife Julia Hennein."

"Doctor accused of raping a minor, commits suicide."

"Doctor commits suicide after killing husband, two kids."

"Bangor doctor who lost husband to suicide hopes to erase stigma attached to depression."

"Doctor who backed controversial operation on child commits suicide."

"Doctor commits suicide at Danville parking garage."

"Madhya Pradesh – woman doctor commits suicide."

"Doctor's suicide in wake of accusations shakes Mammoth Lakes."

"Doctor commits suicide in Lucknow."

"Did hospital politics lead to physician suicide?"

"Doctor dies, son lives, after she injects both with drug."

"Doctor at crux of stunting debate kills self."

"Doctor falls to death from staff quarters."

Chapter 4: The Long History of Physician Suicide

We must not feel exposed or ashamed when a physician kills herself. Our collective response should be a humane one and a call to arms. Our work needs to be at least twofold. We need to launch a supportive approach to the survivors, that is, the huge number of people who are left behind when a doctor takes his life. And we need to redouble our efforts to understand why this particular physician died and to bolster our research into physician suicide. When we ponder the stigma that continues to haunt suicidal individuals and their families in our society, and armed with the knowledge that most people who kill themselves are mentally ill, I have to believe that the culture of medicine, and the house of medicine in particular, need to be at the vanguard of eradicating the stigma and silence associated with suicide. As physicians we need to speak out.

By going public, the culture of medicine honors the individual who has died (as is done in the obituary sections of medical journals). It also communicates unashamedly to the world that we have a problem on our hands and we're doing something about it. In my mind, this will heighten the esteem in which we're held, not sully it.

Here is an example of an honest and dignified tribute to a deceased physician Dr. Judith Anne Hardy from the British Medical Journal October 17, 1998:

General practitioner Basingstoke,1989-98 (b 1951; q Cambridge/St Thomas's 1975; DRCOG, DCH), died, having taken her own life, on 17 June 1998. She spent three years at Mandeville Hospital in Jamaica and she recalled fondly posts in chest medicine, obstetrics and gynaecology, and paediatrics. Her first principal post was in Saffron Walden, moving to Bramley near Basingstoke in 1989. She became a senior partner in January 1998. A sensitive person, she went out of her way to welcome newcomers. She became the driving force in developing the practice,

*expanding the staff and services and moving to purpose built premises.
Judith was modest and self effacing, unaware of her genuine abilities. In
the later years she was haunted by episodes of depression, which,
unresponsive to medication, were unpredictable and finally overwhelming.
She leaves a husband and two sons.*

NEGLECTED INSIGHTS

Despite the fact that doctors have been dying from suicide for a very long
time and there have been articles in the medical literature concerning
physician suicide for well over a century, how much more enlightened are
we today than a generation or more ago?

> *"The greatest obstacle to tackling the mental health issues in doctors is
> stigma. When my father passed, several physicians – his colleagues and
> friends at the hospital – suggested that we - my mother and my brother
> and me - that we cover this up. That we don't tell the world that it was a
> suicide. I said 'No, we are not going to do that, we are telling the truth.
> This is a derangement of a body organ that killed him'".*

The words of Frank Watanabe, whose father, Dr. August "Gus"
Watanabe, while in the throes of a massive depression, killed himself
at the age of 67 on June 9, 2009.

We can only speculate as to what might have prompted Dr. Watanabe's
grieving colleagues to think as they did. Were they wanting to protect their
respected colleague's privacy? Perhaps. His reputation? If so, the implication
is that one's reputation might be sullied by suicide as opposed to cancer or a
heart attack. Or was their thought process rooted in a sense of guilt and a
need to protect the storied image of medicine, to perpetuate the belief that
doctors don't do what lay people do?

I respect the Watanabe family for telling it like it is, for stating that the loss of their beloved father/husband to suicide was the result of a medical condition. He deserves that dignity, and they deserve the right to grieve authentically and without shame.

"I believe in my heart that he would want us to help others by telling his story."

The words of Scott Watanabe, son of Dr. Watanabe

The family's openness in speaking about Dr. Watanabe's sad death is shining a light on what so many of us in the mental health professions and the physician health movement are trying to do. By bringing suicide out of the medical closet, so to speak, they are joining us in our efforts to learn from these premature deaths and to sharpen our diagnostic and therapeutic tools.

The Watanabes are leading by example. I hope that all physicians tempted to cover up the suicide of a dear doctor friend or colleague will think twice about doing that. I believe that most people respect truth and transparency. Openness about suicide in the medical field will help us gain respect – not diminish it. And we have the love and support of our patients who want us to thrive and take care of ourselves.

THE IRONY OF TAKING YOUR OWN LIFE

About 5 years ago, I was invited by the managing editor of a psychiatric periodical to write a short piece on suicide in psychiatrists. Her invitation was prompted by the news that a psychiatrist friend of friends had recently taken his own life. She told me over the phone that the thought of psychiatrists ending their lives was new to her. And very puzzling. I'm paraphrasing what she said to me: "I'm not a doctor or mental health professional. But I just assumed that because you guys are trained in recognizing and treating depression that if you got feeling depressed yourself you would go see someone and get treated. And I also thought that you're sort of at an advantage over us because you know what to look for and who to call. I had no idea that it's a lot more complicated than that".

Dr. SA Knopf wrote the following in 1923:

> *"It is really pathetic that among the members of the profession whose prime objectives are to preserve life…there should be the greatest number of suicides of all the professional classes".*[23]

Fast forward seventy-five years and see how far we've come in terms of understanding. These are the words of Carla Fine again:

> *"We have this belief that physicians have chosen that profession to continue and sustain and protect life…and when a physician kills himself or kills herself, it is very very confusing…because it's almost as if…if they're giving up…what's that mean for the rest of us?"*[24]

After my medical school roommate, Bill, killed himself, I remember telling myself "This doesn't make any sense. You work so hard in high school to get into premed, then you study even harder over the next two years to make the cut, only to pack it in a few short months later?" Nowadays the preparation is even longer, requiring at minimum a three- or four-year undergraduate degree before even applying to medical school. The competition for coveted spots is fierce, and gaining acceptance can evoke a mix of ecstasy, pride, relief, disbelief, humility, and terror. It is hard to conclude that anything other than mental illness could drive such an unfathomable final act in individuals so fortunate and privileged.

THE PHYSICIAN AS CARETAKER OF LIFE

Because physicians are expected to respect, protect, and preserve life, it is hard to come to terms with the knowledge that a doctor has taken her life.

CHAPTER 4: THE LONG HISTORY OF PHYSICIAN SUICIDE

The late Dr. Sherwin Nuland, noted surgeon and author of *How We Die,* wrote the following as a way of explaining why physicians react with such indifference and lack of compassion to suicide:

> *"Something about acute self-destruction is so puzzling to the vibrant mind of a man or woman whose life is devoted to fighting disease that it tends to diminish or even obliterate empathy. Medical bystanders, whether bewildered and frustrated by such an act, or angered by its futility, seem not to be much grieved at the corpse of a suicide"*[25]

Dr. Nuland wrote those words to describe the reaction of physicians assembled in the pathology lab of the medical examiner's office. I am taking some liberty in using his words to explain the reaction of *some* physicians when they learn of an individual, especially a fellow physician, who has died of suicide.

Are Dr. Knopf, Ms Fine, and Dr. Nuland suggesting something bigger here, a fundamental truth that extends beyond what we expect as patients when we put ourselves in the hands of our respective doctors? Historically, physicians have been linked with the clergy and educators (doctor meaning teacher) as esteemed professionals with responsibility to others. As a society, we live with the belief that physicians are not like us, frightened and vulnerable to life's maladies and traumas, that they will always be there to comfort and care for us. Therefore, a physician's suicide is too paradoxical a concept for us to contemplate.

And even with all their medical knowledge, it is still a struggle for some physicians to grasp or justify another doctor's taking his own life. Here are the words of a physician in his thirties, a physician who attended a bereavement group that I facilitated in a small midwestern town after a beloved surgeon killed himself a few years ago:

"I'm kind of struggling with the ethics of this...as you know I'm probably one of the most progressive and open minded docs in this community...look at the patients in my practice and look at my marriage to Ralph...but do we really have the right to kill ourselves?"

And what about patients' feelings?

"After I heard of Dr. Hansbrough's death, it blew me away. This guy changed thousands of lives; he helped thousands of people over his career...and nobody knew that he was having struggles...that's the sad thing about the whole thing...my wife was pregnant with a fourth baby and...we instantly decided 'you know what?'...we're going to name him after John...after John Hansbrough."

The words of "Mike" a burn victim, treated by Dr. John Hansbrough, burn surgeon who died by suicide in 2001 when he was fifty five years old.[26]

"My father's memorial service...it meant a lot for people to come. There were patients there who were devastated, some who called later. They loved him. Rochester is very conservative. His death was public. The newspaper reported that he died by suicide.

Words of Sally Heckel, mentioned earlier in Chapter 1, describing the service for her father, Dr. George Heckel.

"At my brother's memorial service a patient came up to my father. He was crying...he told my dad that Gary (not his real name) had offered to pay for his transplant. There were many of Gary's patients there. They were very touched by his death. One patient purchased and named a memorial star in his honor and sent it to my mother and me. One of his

patients who had moved away to another state wrote us a beautiful letter of thanks for the amazing care that he gave to her."

Words of the sister of a physician who took his own life.

There is not a lot of information available about how patients react to the news that their physician has taken his own life. In fact, if the cause of death is not public knowledge, many patients are never told the truth. They are simply left to speculate, and that can be unsettling. The doctor who steps in to take over the practice will try to avoid questions regarding cause of death and, if asked, avoid answering directly. For some, it may be a question of protecting their deceased colleague's privacy. For others it may be that they think knowing the truth would be traumatic for the patient. And some physicians, in the midst of their own grief, are simply unable to discuss it.

At the funeral for a former patient of mine who took his own life, the minister invited anyone who wished to say a few words to come up to the front of the church. This is what one man had to say:

"I'm a patient of Dr. _____. I'm sorry I cannot say 'I was a patient.' I cannot use the past tense. My doctor saved my life..." As he choked and struggled for words, he stopped and began to sob uncontrollably...two attendants helped him back to his seat.[27]

Patients who have lost their physician to suicide do indeed have a host of thoughts, feelings, and opinions. Here are some of their statements:

- "When I found out that my ex-psychiatrist had killed himself I was really upset, but I didn't cut myself. I felt I owed him that. It's because of him that I don't do that anymore. The weird thing is, I fired him because I thought he really wasn't helping me. It took me a couple of years to see that I am a bit better. The bottom line is that I killed him; I live with that guilt. I thought he was cold and didn't give a shit. Now I think that I wore him down with my phone calls at night and on the weekends. I guess he was really hurting inside with demons. I know he also had other patients like me too."

- "My family doctor was more like a friend to me than a doctor. She really, really cared about me as a person, not just someone with aches and pains. She always took the time to ask about my kids, and especially my mom, who has Alzheimer's. I think she was like this with all her patients. I can't believe she's gone. And in such a sad way."

- "When I heard the rumor that Dr. Reed had killed himself I was shocked, like everyone else. But suicide always kind of kicks you in the gut. I didn't really know him. He operated on me – a knee replacement about five years ago. And he did a great job. But then I got thinking about him and remembered something that I don't think I would have even remembered if he was still alive. Like he was really kind of funny. I asked him if he thought I'd ever play golf again, and without missing a beat he said 'Of course, I'm going to use the Arnold Palmer artificial knee on you. But you have to promise not to tell anyone,' His tone was oh so serious. We shook on it. He looked me in the eye and then winked. I smiled. He smiled. It was kind of intimate in a way. I like that."

- "I'm trying to adjust to my new dermatologist. He's really nice and he's certainly competent but I miss Dr. Levy. Funny, when she went on medical leave I really didn't give it a lot of thought, like the reason is none of my business, she'll be back soon and so forth. But then when I called the office to book my semi-annual visit and I was told that she wouldn't be coming back and that she had died, I really thought I was going to faint. I remember blurting something out like, 'Oh my god, what was it, an accident? Cancer? She was so young.' The receptionist calmly said that it was personal and that Dr. Johns would be my new doctor. Over the next couple of days, I heard from a friend of a friend that Dr. Levy had committed suicide. I felt sick all over again. But like before, I thought, well this is none of my business. But I'll never forget my first visit with Dr. Johns. I was really nervous. I tried to be nice. He didn't bring Dr. Levy up so I did. I said something like 'I am so sorry to hear about Dr. Levy. She was my doctor for quite a few years. I can't really believe she's gone.' He was all business and said 'Our office has a policy to keep the personal lives of all staff strictly private.' Then he returned to examining me. In all honesty, I wasn't really trying to probe. I just wanted to express my feelings, like a condolence. I don't really fault him for his manner. It must be tough trying to replace someone who was so well liked and died so tragically."

- "When my internist killed himself I was shocked and very sad, but strangely not surprised. He had been my doctor for decades, but I noticed over the past couple of years that he seemed stressed. He was getting forgetful and seemed kind of distant or lost in thought when I saw him. He was still friendly and kind but a bit weary. I remember thinking that he's getting up there in years and, like all of us of a certain age, I thought he might be retiring soon. I almost brought it up because he had a younger associate whom I had seen from a distance, and I thought I'd be comfortable with him if Dr. Boxer did retire. Then I read in the newspaper obituary section that his wife had died. I felt kind of sad for him, and I could identify since I lost my wife about ten years ago and know how hard that is. Then a couple of months later I read another article that featured his son, a junior researcher at our local college who had just accepted a big promotion at an Ivy League university across the country. When I was in to see him for a checkup I almost brought these things up, but I didn't think it was my place. I'm so sorry I didn't. I didn't know this would be my last visit and I'd never see him again. Kind of weird in a way, but I'm wondering whether if I had kind of commiserated with him a bit, maybe he wouldn't have done what he did. But who am I? Just a patient, not a friend. But I just feel sad. You doctors give so much to your patients. Do you really take care of yourselves? And do you watch out for each other?"

Those sobering words remind me of the beautifully crafted essay, "The Patient Examines the Doctor," by Anatole Broyard.

"I think that the doctor can keep his technical posture and still move into the human arena. The doctor can use his science as a kind of poetic vocabulary instead of using it as a piece of machinery...I don't expect my doctor to sound like Oliver Sacks, but I do expect some willingness to make contact, some suggestion of availability." [28]

Even though Broyard was craving an emotional connection with his urologist and was not worried about the well-being of his physician, his words indicate that patients do indeed notice their doctors, think about them, and worry about them. The patient's role, however, is not clearly defined. Is it appropriate to speak up? To reach out? To reverse roles and take care of the caretaker? The regrets and "if onlys" that are so ubiquitous after almost all suicides also plague patients whose doctors have taken their own lives.

A DOCTOR TO THE VERY END

It is noteworthy that some physicians are dressed as doctors when they kill themselves. Or they choose their medical office as the setting in which to die. Or they kill themselves at the hospital where they work. Or they choose a medical means of ending their lives.

Carla Fine, mentioned earlier, found her physician husband in his office when she went to check on him because he didn't return home from work. She writes:

> *"I had found him lying on his examining table, covered with blood. The room was a mess. Empty bottles of Thiopental were strewn on the floor, along with discarded needle packets, plastic tubing, and several Milky Way wrappers. The IV pole was upright, tethered to Harry's waist by his black leather belt."*[29]

A patient of mine who killed herself while out on pass from our inpatient psychiatric unit was found dead in her apartment from an intravenous injection of a toxic chemical. She had changed from her street clothes that she wore home from the hospital and put on surgical scrubs.

A woman whom I interviewed for this book told me that her husband killed himself in the on-call room for doctors in the hospital where he worked. Another woman I spoke to lost her physician brother to suicide. The newspaper reported that he "fell" 17 stories from the hospital where he worked. Media outlets in large urban settings have reported on physicians dying by plunges from hospital roofs or higher floors. One woman I interviewed told me that her husband was found dead in the chapel of the hospital where he worked.

This may all be coincidence or is it? Could the means of death or the setting of death have medical meaning? That in that moment of time, the individual is really in the role of physician. In an environment that symbolizes so much of one's training and experience. A setting that until now has brought gratification in serving others. A milieu of helping patients, in doing good work, in defining purpose and having meaning. We can only hope that the doctor has found some good memories and comfort in those lonely final moments of life.

CHAPTER 5

STRESS, BURNOUT, PSYCHIATRIC ILLNESS AND LOSS

Medical practice has always been stressful, but recently, changes in record-keeping, insurance, and technological advances have made it more stressful and frustrating than ever before. Many of today's physicians have made it clear that they would be happy if they could just practice what they were trained to do – look after sick people – instead of having to contend with piles of paper work, keeping up with documentation, mastering electronic health record technology, fighting with insurance companies, staying abreast of the latest medical and scientific advances, and, in many cases coping with diminishing reimbursement for their services, all of which cut into the time they get to spend with their patients. Many confess that they are no longer providing the compassion and basic counseling they once did. Some admit that they have to see more and more patients to keep up with their expenses and overhead. Most abhor and detest having to account to "bean counters."

In an atmosphere that is becoming increasingly litigious, some are sick of practicing defensive medicine. Many are tired, bitter and demoralized. Some look forward to early retirement or consider leaving medicine to pursue another, less demanding and more rewarding career. Examples include opening up a small business, running a B&B, farming, selling real estate, going back to school and more.

The compounding of all these stresses means that burnout has become epidemic in the world of medicine. There are countless articles in our medical journals and blogs, and increasingly in newspapers and weekly magazines, about burnout among doctors. What is less well known and understood about burnout is that it can contribute to suicide among doctors. As one prospective patient put it when he called me:

> *"Hi Dr. Myers, this is Dr. James calling. I've been feeling kind of burned out lately, like for the past nine months or so. I can hardly stand my work anymore and this is kind of new for me. I'm in general practice and I really used to love it until the past several months. But I'm also wondering if I've got a depression going on. How do you tell the difference? So I'd like to come to see you as a patient. Is this something you think you can help me sort out?*

So what exactly is burnout? It is a state of emotional exhaustion, depersonalization (lack of feeling for others), and a diminished sense of personal accomplishment. Put another way, doctors who are burned out complain that they are used up emotionally and have nothing left to give their patients, medical colleagues, and staff. They are running on empty. They have become numb and feel detached from the symptoms and suffering of their patients. They have lost that quality of caring, that sense of empathy that attracted them to medicine in the first place. And finally, they no longer feel that they are helping others or that their efforts are working. At the end of the day they do not go home feeling that their work has meaning or purpose.

Burnout has many dimensions – psychological, physical, spiritual and more – but in the simplest of terms, it is an erosion of the soul. And that is an awful feeling, one that alarms and saddens doctors, who seriously question why they went into medicine in the first place. Or, if this is a major departure from the way they felt a few months or a year or two ago, they are puzzled and confused. They wonder why they don't want to go to work in the morning or why they now find challenging patients daunting or why they want to get certain patients out of the office as fast as they can. They know they are retreating from human interaction; they avoid asking questions they fear might trigger a cascade of feelings or conflicts they no longer want to hear. Some become afraid that they will say or do something very unprofessional (like speaking sarcastically, being physically rough during an examination, uttering insulting remarks or using curse words), which can become frightening and paralyzing. Others worry about making a mistake, not listening carefully and attentively enough, neglecting an important part of the physical examination, not ordering the right tests, missing the correct diagnosis, and not prescribing the best treatment. And their fears are not invalid. It is fact that burned out physicians do make more errors.

The term "burnout" is bandied about so much among doctors these days that it is almost a badge of honor to be burned out. It means that you are a hard-working physician trying to survive in today's medical workforce. Jokes are made but it isn't really a joking matter. No doctor wants patient care to suffer and no one wants to make mistakes, but there is some comfort in knowing that you're not alone, that your colleagues feel the same way. And because burnout is not included in our list of psychiatric diagnoses, there is no stigma attached to it, which makes it easier for doctors to accept and talk about than being diagnosed with depression or anxiety or a drinking problem.

Because burnout is essentially an occupational hazard, there is a tendency to blame the system for the problem. This makes sense. Burned out doctors rightfully argue that they are just trying to do their job, trying to help patients. In fact, there is some evidence that shows that the most sensitive and conscientious doctors are more prone to burnout precisely because they care so deeply about their mission. They really want the best for their patients. The paradox is that their unselfishness and kindness backfire and they end up getting sick themselves. Physicians with a more businesslike attitude tend to be more resilient to the slings and arrows of today's medical industry. Studies are now underway to determine the usefulness of a "prevent burnout toolkit" to help doctors survive in the workplace. This includes things like meditation, yoga, physical exercise, onsite day-care, reducing the volume of paper work, improved electronic health records, tips for balancing life more, flex time, shorter work weeks, and regular group discussions of complicated patient encounters.

WHEN "BURN OUT" IS REALLY A MOOD DISORDER

DEPRESSION

Just 4 weeks ago, my father, an internationally-known and respected radiologist, died by his own hand in Seattle. He was a 66 year old Ultrasound Radiologist, and Professor at the University of Washington. His colleagues tell me he was a giant in the field of Ultrasound, and one of the important early pioneers in that field. He taught innumerable interns and residents, wrote many landmark articles on the topic, and was instrumental in helping to pass legislation in Washington State to limit health care costs via imaging. In short, he had a legendary medical career.

Despite all these accomplishments, he suffered from a low self-image and was easily triggered into severe depression and anxiety when something made him doubt his skills and stability. In the last weeks of his life, because of a stressful episode at work, he came to believe that he was a

*fraud, that he should retire, and that he had done nothing of value in his
life. Clearly, my father's sense of himself was built on his accomplishments.
Any event that might suggest a flaw in those accomplishments was enough
to make the bottom fall out of his confidence, enough to send him into a
suicidal despair. To me, this is proof that depression can affect anyone,
and can completely alter that individual's sense of reality.*

Email received from Dan Bree September 29, 2010, regarding his
father Dr. Robert Bree

Most people (85 to 90 percent to be exact) who die by suicide are in the
midst of a psychiatric illness at the time of their death. Physicians are no
exception. They may not even know that they are sick. They know they
don't feel well, but they don't necessarily know they are suffering from a
mental illness. Or even if they do, they may not be receiving any treatment.
Or they may not be fully cooperating with the treatment that's been
prescribed. Or they may not be receiving the right treatment. Or they have
concluded – erroneously, and often prematurely – that the treatment they
are receiving will not help them, that psychiatric treatments do not work, or
that their situation is hopeless and not treatable, period. Just prior to
attempting suicide, most individuals are suffering from tunnel vision,
narrowed thinking, cognitive restriction. All these terms describe a
dangerous and life-threatening thinking process that is rigid, despairing,
unwavering, and blind to life-affirming options.

We now know quite a lot about the most common psychiatric illnesses
suffered by physicians, illnesses that, if left untreated or inadequately
treated, put them at risk for self-harm. Depression is number one. The rates
of depression among medical students and physicians are known to be a bit
higher than those of the general public. But depression is also a very
treatable illness, much like diabetes and heart disease, and state-of-the-art

73

treatment prevents many depressed people from killing themselves every year. That said, not all physicians, even with good or at least adequate treatment, survive. What follows is a suicide note written by a physician "Arthur" that conveys not only his anguish but a fierce determination to escape the horror.

> *"All I do is suffer each and every day. Every moment is pain or numbness. How long can one go without pleasure? I guess these will really be my last words…It's over. Finally over. I will do it now. I have nothing left. My mind is wracked with thoughts. I can't concentrate or perform at work…I am getting very drowsy. I will likely fall asleep soon. I hope I have taken enough to finish this. I would not want to be revived or survive through this. It would only make life more horrific to deal with. Please do not resuscitate me if alive when found."[30]*

BIPOLAR ILLNESS

In her brilliant piece "To Know Suicide", psychologist, researcher, teacher and one who lives with bipolar illness, Dr. Jamison captures, with frightening eloquence, the awful place that individuals reside in when they are severely depressed and suicidal. She explains how in many depressed bipolar individuals, an agitated mania accompanies the state of despair only to make matters more intolerable and further driving the need to end it all.[31]

Like the suicide note of "Arthur" above, here is a letter written by a woman physician who was diagnosed with bipolar disorder years earlier while in medical school. It too captures her severe anguish and terror about losing her mental stability:

> *"Feel flat all the time – mornings worst – trying to force myself to be cheerful but feels FORCED like behind a glass screen losing touch with other people – no connection, speech forced, smiles forced, words hollow*

everything's an effort no drive or motivation…Feel useless as a mother, as a wife, as a woman…see no hope for the future…focusing on my precious baby Freya – she means everything to me, I desperately want to be a good mother to her but I'm starting to feel that I'm failing her in a big way, that everyone can see I'm a useless mother that I'm no good…I've been down this road before, don't want to breakdown or end up on psychiatric ward having ECT. Want to avoid that at all cost – I've got my baby to think about. Got to keep going for her she's everything to me, more than life itself. She needs me + I'm going to be there for her, whatever it takes.

Excerpts from Daksha's Last Note, the suicide note written by Dr. Daksha Emson. She and her daughter, aged three months, died following an extended suicide (murder-suicide wherein people dying by suicide do not see the other as separate from themselves) on October 9, 2000, in London.[32]

I interviewed her husband David Emson both over the telephone in 2015 and in person in London in the fall of 2016. When asked for his suggestions about what could be learned from his wife's tragic death and what could be done differently, he had this to say about the role of doctors' spouses:

Spouses should be included as far as practically possible in the care of their partner, they should be acknowledged as their 'unofficial carer' and not viewed as an appendage or positioned on the periphery of any planned care and treatment programmes; spouses should be seen as another resource in monitoring the health of their partner, to be primed in recognizing signs of a relapse of their partner's illness, and in effect be the eyes and ears of the responsible medical officer in the interim period between regular and planned appointments.

Mr Emson's words gave me pause. I took away an important message from these words and my musings, a revelation that confirms so much of what I've been describing earlier: this illness enshrouds and takes over the person's life with a chokehold – it is folly and naive to think that a physician victim would have the power or insight to ask for help and not harm himself. I realize that to many mental health professional readers this is a 'no brainer' but I say it here because not all therapists know this. They do believe that their physician patient's medical education and training are ascendant and that even facing despair she will call for help and articulate what she's experiencing.

Bipolar illness (what used to be called manic-depressive disorder) is a type of mood disorder defined by an alternating pattern of high and low emotional states, but you only have to experience one episode of an elevated state to have the illness. Although less common than depression, the risk of attempting suicide and dying by suicide is greater. And, once again, it is very treatable, usually with mood stabilizing medications. Most individuals respond nicely and lead healthy, productive lives.

The problem is that the milder form of the illness, called bipolar II type, can be missed because the high or manic episode may be brief and the elevated spirits, overly confident thinking, or self-absorbed behavior are not seen as unusual.

Doctors who have bipolar illness seem to live with more internalized stigma (they are hard on themselves and feel flawed and unacceptable), which can make it that much harder for them to accept the diagnosis and commit to proper treatment. Like bipolar patients in general, those physicians who do accept the fact that they have an illness that requires lifelong treatment, keep all their doctor's appointments, take their medications as prescribed, lead a healthy lifestyle and accept the love and support of their families and friends, will do well.

CHAPTER 5: STRESS, BURNOUT, PSYCHIATRIC ILLNESS AND LOSS

The key message here is that psychiatric illnesses are always hard to accept, and often even harder for doctors than for the general public. It is a process that takes time. Some move along this journey faster than others. But most physicians, over time, do reach that place of acceptance. Some have even gone public with their stories, and some of these have survived suicide attempts. Some are fluent spokespeople for the mental health movement and the value of our treatments. Most have shed the shackles of stigma that delayed or derailed their ability to embrace the care that they needed. Their stories are powerful and persuasive, courageous and generous. They grieve their brothers and sisters in medicine whose suffering became unbearable and who ended their lives. They want this to stop.

One such person is Dr. Suzanne Vogel-Scibilia, a psychiatrist and past president of the National Alliance on Mental Illness. Her bipolar illness began when she was fifteen years old. She is a tireless advocate for the rights of the mentally ill and is deeply committed to education and advocacy. Another, although not a physician, is psychologist Dr. Kay Redfield Jamison quoted above. Her many books, especially *An Unquiet Mind: A Memoir of Moods and Madness*[33] and *Night Falls Fast: Understanding Suicide,*[34] and her lectures and articles in the popular press have helped countless people living with a mood disorder – and their families. She is a great friend of medicine and is one of the most sought after lecturers at medical schools and medical conferences across the country.

WHAT ABOUT DRUGS AND ALCOHOL?

Alcohol and drugs are both substances that can lead to addiction in people, especially those who are genetically vulnerable. They cannot drink socially or in moderation. Alcoholism runs in families and medical families are no exception. In fact, a good number of medical students are adult children of alcoholics whose decision to study medicine may, at least in part, result from that fact.

But why does alcoholism lead to suicide in some doctors? I asked the daughter of a physician who killed himself for her insights on this.

For as long as I can remember when I was growing up, I saw my father as having a love affair with alcohol. He was always in a good mood when he came home, and after a perfunctory hello to my mom and me, he headed straight to the liquor cabinet. I always thought he enjoyed his work (he was an anesthesiologist) and that's why he was so happy. But no, he was happy because he was now free to get shit-faced. In fact, he never drank when he was on call – I'm pretty sure of that – so he was even happier, like almost giddy, when that long tour of duty was over and he was released and didn't have to help sick people. I think scotch was his best friend, like a companion, because he really didn't like people and preferred sitting alone in the den with a drink, reading and watching TV. He was really a loner. And this became even more obvious when my mother left him. He never said much or showed much reaction. He may actually have been relieved because then he could be all alone without having to wonder if maybe he should sit with her in the room where she was watching TV by herself.

I was away at college when he killed himself. I was shocked but not surprised. I think in hindsight that he probably took the divorce harder than we all thought. He may have been relieved at first, but I think now that he got worse. Like, pathologically lonely and isolated. He had begun to let himself go – and the house was a mess – like you see in people who are slowly developing Alzheimer's. I don't know how he managed to keep working right up until the end. But it's all so sad. In fact, I think his whole life was sad. I guess he enjoyed being a doctor, but he never talked about his work. He was so private. Such an introvert. It's also kind of surprising to me – but I'm not in a health field at all – that he was a

*doctor who never saw a doctor for himself – ever – or went to an internist
or AA or saw a psychiatrist or psychologist. Why would a doctor decide to
end his life without thinking – hmmmmm this is pretty serious – maybe
I'm depressed, maybe I should talk to a shrink, maybe I need some pills
or something, maybe the scotch is making me worse…*

WHEN DEPRESSION IS COMBINED WITH DRINKING

When a mood disorder is combined with a substance use problem, it is
called a comorbid condition or a dual diagnosis disorder. Both problems are
serious and require specific and contemporaneous treatment. Here is an
example from my private practice:

*Under my breath, I am reciting "Adonay natan, ve'Adonay lakah; yehi
shem Adonay me'vorkakh. The Lord has given, the Lord has taken
away, blessed be the name of the Lord."*

*This is the first sentence of the Jewish prayer for a patient who has died. I
am in the intensive care unit and my patient Gord has just been taken off
life support. He looks like he's at peace. I am there with his sister and his
parents. The neurologist attending him is a classmate of his from medical
school. I marvel at his composure, his gentleness and his kindness to the
four of us. Thirty-six hours earlier Gord was found by his neighbor
hanging from his bike rack on the balcony of his apartment. EMS rushed
him to the hospital. He never regained consciousness. I reflected on my five
years of being his psychiatrist - and his bravery. Gord had an awful
treatment-resistant depression (colloquially "a nasty depression") that
challenged not just me but the several other psychiatrists who worked with
him through his many hospitalizations, multiple medication trials, courses
of electroconvulsive therapy, and different kinds of psychotherapy. But all*

of this was complicated by his drinking. Despite valiant efforts and lots of resources to fight his addiction, he could not sustain sobriety. He was forty-four when he died. He had fought the good fight.

Today we know a great deal about the neurobiological underpinnings of addiction, all of which explain the cravings, the tolerance that develops, the inability to stop drinking, the withdrawal symptoms, and the continued use against one's better judgment. But when asked about their drinking, very few physicians provide a scientifically accurate response. They say they drink to fight the depression (which doesn't work, because alcohol is itself a depressant chemical). Or they drink to calm the anxiety that often comes with depression. Or they drink to counteract the side-effects of some antidepressant medications. Or they drink out of loneliness or habit or to fit in socially with their friends. And doctors with bipolar illness may drink either when they're a bit high (because they're a bit reckless about everything) or a bit low, for a supposed "pick me up" effect.

What is most important is that the risk of suicide is higher in those with a comorbid condition.

WHEN PHYSICIANS HAVE A CHRONIC MEDICAL ILLNESS

Like people in general, medical illnesses can be devastating to physicians and the stress may be very high. Doctors who have been diagnosed with chronic diseases that slowly get worse – like amyotrophic lateral sclerosis (Lou Gehrig's Disease), multiple sclerosis, severe congestive heart failure, chronic obstructive pulmonary disease, autoimmune disorders – may find themselves thinking about suicide. Chronic disease is characterized by loss of physical and/or mental abilities and often of independence. Coupled with all of this – is the loss of one's professional position and stature in his medical community, the reputation that one enjoyed, the busyness of one's working day, and the gratification of serving others. There is major erosion of the doctor's professional identity and pride. He feels marginalized and very alone.

My father was diagnosed with cancer 5 or 6 years before he died. He was treated with radiation and chemotherapy. The origin of the tumor was never known. But he had many side-effects of his cancer treatment. Especially hard were his wheezing and he wasn't able to exercise as much as before he got sick. This was a big loss for him. Then he got a recurrence of the cancer. I wonder if this was on his mind before his suicide, that he would need treatment again and it would be intolerable and unendurable. I know there were other stresses in his life. And he had a lifelong depressive streak which had a lot to do with his family background, especially his parents living through and surviving the Great Depression. I think my dad felt a lot of humiliation. I understand his suicide now as protecting his family from his decline. He bowed out when he thought it was necessary to do so. He killed himself as a blessing, not a curse. But it's still so very sad that he's gone. He'd be very proud of his three kids.

Some words from my interview with Dr. David Greenspan, a psychiatrist. He lost his father, also a psychiatrist, to suicide in 1988.

Serious medical illness in physicians, especially with a poor prognosis and/or accompanying pain, may play a major role in the decision to take one's life. However, because unrecognized and untreated depression often accompanies these illnesses, it is essential that all patients diagnosed with such disorders undergo a thorough psychiatric assessment. Too often depression is paid lip service "Well, of course you're depressed, I would be too if I was living with what you've got". It is seen as a normal psychological response to an assault on the body (which may be true in the beginning) but what is missed is that the mood disorder now has a life of its own (with obsessive and gloomy thinking, incessant worry, poor appetite, weight loss and disturbed sleep) and must be treated. With improved spirits and clearer thinking suicide loses its urgency.

WHAT ABOUT PERSONALITY DISORDERS?

A personality disorder is a life-long condition that can place sufferers at odds with other people. For doctors those people may be professors, peers in medical school, training directors in residency, attending physicians who teach them, employers and others in authority in the medical workplace, but also family members, other loved ones, and sometimes their patients. Those with these kinds of character traits or difficulties can be quite critical of others, have trouble seeing their role in a conflict, and tend to blame the other person. Much like adolescents who are masters at playing their parents off against each other, doctors with character flaws can cause a lot of friction and tension between key people in the medical setting. Some are ultrasensitive, suspicious of peers or authority figures, and tend to feel uneasy or victimized. Some are quite narcissistic, self-serving, and disdainful of others. They have trouble being team-players and may be hypercritical and litigious.

Most doctors with personality problems do not generally kill themselves. Suicide is always due to a confluence of forces coming together and rendering the individual overwhelmed and despairing. Therefore, those with personality disorders who are most at risk also tend to have some type of comorbid illness. For example, a physician who has both bipolar illness and a personality disorder might have more trouble staying well than a doctor with bipolar illness alone. His personality might create problems for him at work and he might lose his job, which could destabilize his mood so that he doesn't respond as well to his medications. Or, because of his personality flaws, he might not trust his psychiatrist or adhere to the treatment plan. He might drop out of treatment, stop taking his medication, and he gets worse. Then instead of going to another doctor he might start to self-medicate with samples from his office or begin drinking to lift his mood or calm his anxiety. At that point his wife might get upset and frustrated, and eventually she might leave. That might cause him to feel even more lost and increase his isolation. He might even become psychotic and in a frenzied, agitated state be unable to see any way out other than suicide.

Doctors with personality disorders are generally able to withstand quite a lot of emotional criticism or psychological assaults. But the strongest self-protective defenses can crumble under the weight of overwhelming stress such as being charged with some kind of abusive behavior, being accused or found guilty of some kind of scientific fraud, cheating, or falsifying information, or being found guilty of misappropriation of funds. They are most dangerous to themselves when they are humiliated because the issue becomes public knowledge, they are not in therapy, and their family and friends have ceased to support them.

ACUTE SUICIDAL AFFECTIVE DISTURBANCE

Although this entity is still being studied and requires a lot of scientific rigor, I include it here because it is a suicide specific problem.[35] And it is perilous without quick recognition and action. As the name suggests it is acute, meaning suicidal thinking and planning builds quickly over hours or days, not weeks or months. The individual may have one or both of the following: marked social alienation (e.g. severe social withdrawal, disgust with others) or self-alienation (self-disgust and feeling like a burden). These symptoms are believed by the person to be intractable and the individual is overly aroused (e.g. can't sleep, has nightmares, is agitated or irritable). This constitutes a psychiatric emergency and anyone feeling this way should be taken to an emergency room immediately and receive a comprehensive psychiatric assessment and observation. This may include being detained against their wishes to ensure safety from self-harm.

Beyond diagnostic labels: The role of everyday loss

Loss is a given of medical practice. But this is not something doctors generally articulate because they are simply too busy to reflect upon or grieve the many losses in their professional life.

- Time spent having coffee or lunch with medical colleagues (because doctors' lounges have all but disappeared from medical centers and clinics)

- The retirement of senior staff who were often mentors and respected figures whom they could discuss challenging patients with

- The deaths of associates and friends whom they remembered briefly at a funeral or memorial service but didn't have time to grieve

- The worsening condition of some of their patients despite good care, and the lack of time to address the psychological aspects of this

- The deaths of patients they have treated over the long term, an inevitable part of medical work that can get to your soul

- A skill set that has become anachronistic and irrelevant in our high-tech medical centers, such as aspects of the hands-on physical exam that are now deemed old-fashioned or time consuming. Physicians actually miss touching their patients! (and we know that patients miss that too!)

Beyond these professional losses there are also losses in the personal
lives of physicians that often get short shrift:

- The worsening health and/or subsequent death of an aging parent.
  This is particularly tough when the parent lives far away and the
  physician does not take enough time away to simply be there for a
  few days or weeks, or perhaps returns to work too quickly after the
  death and feels bitter or shortchanged by the needs of his patients

- The launch of a child who is leaving home to attend college.

- The realization that they are no longer either looking or feeling as
  young as they once did – that age is catching up with them.

- An unexamined marital separation and/or divorce. Too many
  doctors (especially men) move into a new relationship without really
  taking the time to fully understand what happened to the previous
  one.

- Disconnection from siblings who live far away and the realization
  that they are missing many of the milestones in each other's lives.

- Lack of a spiritual or religious anchor in one's life. Whether or not
  the doctor was raised in a religiously observant home, there can be a
  sense that something is missing, and that feels like a loss of some
  kind

When too many of these professional and personal losses pile one upon
the other the aggregate weight – particularly if they are not acknowledged or
expressed – can become too heavy to bear. And that's when the physician,
like anyone else, becomes vulnerable to depression and perhaps to suicide.
In fact, many physicians who have been diagnosed with clinical depression

and helped by medication, don't realize until they're feeling better how much they need to grieve their professional and personal losses.

One patient of mine whom I'll call Dr. Jones, came at the insistence of his wife, Irma, for couples therapy, because, as she said, her husband had stopped talking, and she was feeling more lonely than if she'd actually been alone. Dr. Jones knew that he wasn't, as he put it, "a talker," and thought that perhaps they shouldn't have married in the first place. But he insisted that he wasn't depressed. And, as I soon learned, he was correct. He wasn't clinically depressed, but he was sad, preoccupied, and broken – for very good reasons. His background was punctuated with loss. When he was eleven years old, his older sister and only sibling had died of Reye's Syndrome as a result of having taken aspirin during a bout of chicken pox. This was devastating for his parents, especially his mother who had administered the aspirin. According to Dr.Jones, his mother had never recovered from the loss, and even antidepressants hadn't helped. But that wasn't the worst of it. When he was in college his mother had hanged herself, and five days later when he got off the plane taking him back to college, he was greeted by the police, who told him that his father had shot himself in the heart. "I don't know how I survived that," said Dr. Jones. "I still don't."

It wasn't until he began therapy with me that Dr. Jones realized the degree to which he'd been avoiding examining how much losing his entire family had impacted his life and was now impacting his marriage. Once he began to do that he became much more animated and open with his wife, and they regained their intimacy fairly quickly, both inside and outside the bedroom.

THE ROLE OF RESILIENCE

Resilience is a subject that permeates the medical literature these days. It is defined as a life force that promotes regeneration and renewal in people. It is the ability to confront adversity and still find hope and meaning in one's life. The good news is that most physicians are extremely resilient. It served them well in their early years when they worked hard to get the good grades and the superior MCAT scores that are necessary to get into medical school. Resilience also enabled them to do a significant amount of volunteer work and participate in sports or master a musical instrument while still maintaining their grades. Resilience got them through tough basic sciences in medical school and demanding clinical rotations before earning their MD. In fact, despite the high burnout rates among medical students and physicians, most push through it – or make healthy choices and changes in their life – and bounce back.

Unfortunately, however, resilience is not an absolute guarantee of fitness or protection from suicide. Physicians with a history of stellar resilience can still become self-destructive. Suicidal doctors can no longer fend off the slings and arrows of everyday life as they once did. They feel useless and worthless. And they hurt terribly inside. Once again, recognizing this and getting immediate help is imperative because, with proper treatment, one's normal level of resilience will return as symptoms abate.

THE HARSH REALITY FOR TOO MANY MEDICAL FAMILIES

Several of the families I interviewed for this book highlighted their anxiety and worry about their loved ones before they died. They struggled with the knowledge that all physicians have studied basic psychiatry in medical school and beyond, especially in specialties such as primary care, pediatrics, and psychiatry – and yet, when push came to shove, they did not recognize the degree to which emotional or mental illness had taken over their life. In some cases, their family members pleaded with them to get help. Some even made appointments for them as a couple or a family, doing whatever they could to make it easier, only to have their family member not show up or cancel. They worried not only about the doctor's suffering but also his ability to function. They worried about the safety and medical judgment of their loved one. Was he practicing competent medicine? Might he make a grave error and harm a patient? Some got help from their loved one's doctor colleagues. But others, sadly, found that their requests for help were dismissed or ignored. I have been both moved and humbled by their stories. They are truly advocates on the front lines of the battle to save the lives of doctors.

CHAPTER 6

HOW STIGMA KILLS DOCTORS

"The greatest obstacle to good mental health is stigma. There needs to be greater recognition that depression is a disease with a huge physiological element. This will not only help doctors recognize it in themselves but it will help the broader society as they approach their patients this way."

Mr Watanabe lost his father Dr. August Watanabe to suicide June 9, 2009

In May 2000 I was invited to meet with health professionals in Holland, Michigan, after the chief of staff at their local hospital killed himself. He was a forty-four-year-old surgeon, a devout Christian, and father of four daughters. The Holland community was in shock and reeling from the tragic loss of this very capable and beloved physician. While I was there, I met the doctor's pastor and the pastor's wife, who gave the eulogy at the doctor's funeral. She gave me a printed copy of what she said:

Depression is a silent killer

It does its dark work best when we deny that it exists

Its partner is shame

Together they isolate,

Causing pain that is unbearable,

Distorting our perception of reality until

We are convinced that the world will be better off

Without us.

It causes irrational anger – confusion – fear,

Until one's mind gropes for a way to stop the pain.

Its victims have been among the world's brightest –

Most talented – kindest – most faithful.

And now our brother has succumbed to this terrible disease.

Let us destroy the power of this illness by naming it.

In these few words, she captured the destructive power of depression – the horrific pain, the distorted thinking, the emotional whirlwind, the powerlessness of the sufferer, and the fact that it can affect anyone. But, most important, she pointed out how silence and shame can fuel self-annihilation. And she concluded by exhorting the mourners to "destroy the power of this illness by naming it." She makes the point that too often we dance around the disease of depression by euphemisms like "had a few problems" or "was kind of stressed out."

There are actually two types of stigma: enacted and felt. Although these terms were originally used to describe stigma associated with epilepsy, they have been extended to mental illness. Enacted stigma is exterior and refers to discrimination against people with a psychiatric illness because of their perceived unacceptability or inferiority. Felt stigma is interior and refers to both the fear of enacted stigma and a feeling of shame associated with having a mental illness.[36] I believe that both types are in play when a symptomatic physician begins to wonder if he might have a mental disorder. And among physicians the level of stigma is, in many if not most cases, notably higher than in the general population.

Stigma then fuels denial and the tendency to minimize the severity of their illness, even when a friend, family member, or colleague suggests, however gently and kindly, that they seem different – maybe sad, tired, or withdrawn – and there might be a problem.

It's probably safe to say that virtually no one actually wants to admit that he is suffering from an anxiety or mood disorder or is abusing alcohol or other drugs. Most of us would rather just bury ourselves in our work (or our head in the sand) and simply hope that the problem will go away on its own. And if it doesn't, we wait a while longer, even though we know we should really be reaching out for help. And all these symptoms of denial are that much more entrenched when the person with the problem is a physician.

But because it leads to denial, stigma (or the fear of being stigmatized) can have far more pernicious effects. Stigma kills. I believe it was perceived stigma that killed a patient of mine, a young doctor who ended his life with a lethal injection of potassium chloride he'd been stockpiling. He did this while he was out on a pass from our psychiatric inpatient unit. My hunch is that one of the final determinants in his decision to kill himself had to do with a perceived threat to his professional identity – the fear that he would not be allowed to continue his residency, which was his lifeline to normalcy and security – and to the fulfillment of his dreams. Although no one had said anything like this to him, because of the cognitive impairment that is a symptom of depression, he made a huge assumption that it would happen.

Sadly, this young man's tragedy is as relevant today as it was when he died almost fifteen years ago. Speaking to loved ones, friends, and colleagues who have survived the suicide of a physician, I am constantly struck by the degree to which internalized stigma in the physician loved one was a driving force from behind their death. Several received no treatment at all and ignored or rejected the attempts made by those who cared deeply about them to get them to seek help. I asked the widow of a physician who died of an overdose if her husband might have sought help and didn't tell her, her response was, "I don't think so; we were very close; he didn't keep secrets like that from me." Then, after a long pause, she continued. "Well, I thought he told me everything but obviously I was wrong. He made this very big decision without consulting me."

THE DANGERS OF DENIAL AND DELAY

Although I'm not aware of any scientific research into the length of time physicians, as opposed to the general public, delay seeking help, I do know that many of the survivors I've spoken to told me that they believe their loved one would still be alive if he were not a doctor. We do know that women delay less in going for professional help than men do. Whether this applies to women in medicine is unclear.

We have known for some time that early intervention has a positive effect on treatment and prognosis for psychiatric illnesses in general and depression in particular. Ironically, most physicians, especially primary care doctors, are aware of this and are increasingly screening for depression in their patients but then turn a blind eye to their own symptoms.

Although most doctors will still respond to conventional treatment when they do seek help (or may even start feeling okay with no treatment), some won't. They take longer to get better, may struggle for some time with residual symptoms, and may require the expertise of a psychopharmacologist along with psychotherapy. At worst, prolonged procrastination, puts the patient at risk for prolonged or worsening despondency and demoralization, the sense that this horror is never going away, which can then lead to more and more intense thoughts of suicide.

In addition, practicing medicine when you are not at your best is risky. Errors of commission and omission are a distinct possibility, if not a probability. Cognitive slowing and/or distorted thinking mean you're not as diagnostically and therapeutically sharp as usual. Multitasking is an essential skill in medicine, and you can't do that if you're distracted and unable to concentrate. Memory impairment is a common symptom of depression, which makes it difficult to follow the patient's story and ask the right questions. Confident decision-making is diminished, so you end up hesitating, deliberating or doubting your findings and course of action. Prescription-writing and staying on top of charting, electronic health records, and billing become even more onerous than usual.

In addition, living with untreated psychiatric symptoms puts vulnerable doctors at risk for a range of medical illnesses, including coronary artery disease, high blood pressure, diabetes and other endocrine disorders, musculoskeletal maladies and more. The comorbidity (that I mentioned in the last chapter) is quite serious. And too commonly, physicians slowly increase what was once social use of alcohol so that they now become symptomatic drinkers which can lead to a substance use disorder. A smaller cohort of doctors reverts to street drug usage – marijuana, cocaine, ketamine, heroin. Anesthesiologists, critical care physicians and surgeons may begin to divert narcotic drugs in the workplace (meaning they 'pocket' some of the drug that they prescribe to their patients). They then use the diverted medicine later by injecting themselves. This is dangerous and can kill too.

One danger specific to those with a medical license and a prescription pad is their ability to treat themselves with antidepressants, stimulants, tranquilizers, sleeping pills, and even antipsychotic medications, any or all of which can be extremely dangerous if not properly prescribed and carefully monitored by an objective professional. Clearly, objectivity isn't possible when the prescriber is also the patient. In addition to which, doctors who are not extremely familiar with these types of medication may not know if the drugs are working or if they are developing side effects. They may change the dosage or stop one and start another, which can be extremely hazardous, because they don't have the same medical judgment they would use with their patients.

HOW STIGMA AFFECTS TREATMENT

Even when a physician does recognize that she is ill and seeks professional help, felt stigma can affect the treatment relationship. Doctors who feel ashamed of having a mental illness may be less forthcoming in sharing information with their therapist. They may be embarrassed to disclose key pieces of information about their personal and family history or to talk about certain symptoms such as drinking, previous suicide attempts, or having treated themselves with drug samples from the office. Therefore, the treating psychiatrist (or other therapist) may not get a true picture of how severely ill the doctor patient really is or what is causing the illness.

Even well-intentioned physician-patients may be less likely than non-doctors to stick with the treatment plan, may miss or cancel appointments, and may "forget" to take their medications. Rather than collaborating with their therapist, they may assume a passive attitude and resist engaging in talk therapy, especially when it is explorative digging to get at underlying causes.

Each therapy session they attend or pill they take is a reminder that they are undergoing psychiatric treatment. Because of that, they may quit as soon as they begin to feel better or seduce their therapist into believing that they are "cured", or at least far more improved than they really are.

Then, if they relapse, they are all the more reluctant to return to treatment because they believe and are ashamed that they have failed their psychiatrist and that she will, therefore be angry or disappointed.

CHAPTER 6: HOW STIGMA KILLS DOCTORS

Because their lives have been so defined by achievement, doctors may feel even more uncomfortable than most with the notion of being perceived as a failure, or, even worse, as a burden. I can't even count the number of times doctors who call for an appointment begin by saying, "Sorry to bother you Dr. Myers..." What this tells me is that we need to show these doctors the kind of compassion so many of them are still struggling to give themselves.

Much of their stigma is felt – that is, self-created, but even more sadly, in some instances it is, in fact, enacted. A psychiatrist who had lived with major depression for years, and who happens to be a friend, encountered exactly that kind of stigma when he moved to a new city and had to find a psychiatrist. Although he doesn't announce his condition to the world, neither is he embarrassed or feel diminished by it. Therefore he found the reaction of the first doctor he visited particularly unsettling. This is how he described it to me on the phone:

You know, Mike. I've just moved to [unnamed city] to start my new job. First order of business – get a new psychiatrist to take over my care. I asked around and was given the name of [Dr. Blank], who sees a lot of doctors in town. I was really looking forward to seeing him. Let me tell you what happened. It didn't go well, but now I wonder if that's my fault. You're a former training director so maybe you can help. The visit started out okay but it went south when he asked why I'd never disclosed my illness to my residency training director. I told him I didn't think that was necessary because I was well the entire time, taking my medication and seeing my regular psychiatrist from medical school every six months. But he kept focusing on the fact that I should have revealed my history of depression even before I began my residency. When I asked him to explain why he felt this way, he got really sarcastic and kind of belittling. He said,

"The ethical thing to do is to be transparent. You should have let the training director know that you have a "pre-condition" so that they could keep an eye on you." When I asked him what he meant by that (assuming he meant 'pre-existing condition') he really got upset and accused me of playing dumb. He said something like, "Surely I don't need to explain to you, a psychiatrist, that when a doctor has a history of depression, if it comes back it could affect his work with patients. And that is why when you're in training you should tell the director so he or she can be on 'high alert'" I felt really confused then. And ashamed actually. I am an ethical person. I know my illness well, and so did my psychiatrist at the time. I would have gone on medical leave if my symptoms came back and I was at risk of harming my patients. But this has really upset me. I haven't slept well the last couple of nights, and that's also why my wife agreed that I should call you. What do you think? I wonder now if he was right, that I was kind of fraudulent by not coming out about my illness to the training director."

After consoling my friend, whose mood and self-regard had just taken a nose-dive, I assured him that he had done nothing wrong. There is no obligation to disclose one's personal health history unless there is evidence of impairment at work, or a history of impairment in the past. Thankfully, I succeeded in reassuring him, and afterwards I made a few phone calls and found him a different psychiatrist with whom he had a very good fit.

The good news is that he reached out to me to gain perspective. But many people in his position can't or don't have that option.

A VARIANT OF STIGMA: ALTRUISM VS SELF-INTEREST

There are many physicians who believe it is selfish to focus on yourself. Perhaps this is an unfortunate misinterpretation of the Hippocratic Oath, which states that a physician must always put the needs of his patients ahead of his own, but doctors who hold this belief often struggle with making time for themselves.

What can happen then is that the physician burns out, is emotionally exhausted and not functioning well, but instead of taking time to see his own personal physician, he overcompensates by working even harder, "overgives" to patients, staff, and colleagues, even taking their on-call shifts when they need someone to fill in.

Slowly, over time, he quite naturally becomes more and more tired, and, as a result, his self-regard also plummets. He then works even harder to get approval from others, but that just makes things worse. The more exhausted he becomes, the more he feels depressed, guilty, and despairing. Very sad, but not rare in the world of medicine.

WHEN YOUR FAMILY DOESN'T SUPPORT YOU

When a physician becomes mentally or emotionally ill, it isn't unusual for one or more family members to minimize the problem. They may be judgmental or make light of his symptoms, accuse him of feeling sorry for himself or crying wolf. The reason for this kind of behavior may actually be that these folks are afraid of being stigmatized themselves. They may fear losing their reputation or social image in medical circles, being ostracized or shunned if they are honest with friends or neighbors. So they lie and say that their son is taking a break from his residency and travelling in Asia rather than disclose that he is in a treatment center for cocaine use.

This was the problem faced by one of my patients, a twenty-three-year-old female, African-American medical student who came to me with self-diagnosed depression.

She had been experiencing a low mood every day for about two months, during which time she had also lost almost fifteen pounds, her energy was depleted and, as she put it, "I feel like an old woman. I can't run anymore, only walk, and that even tires me out." She was having trouble both concentrating on and retaining the material she was studying, and now she was awakening every morning at four AM and couldn't get back to sleep. She said that her spirits lifted a bit as the day went on, but she was always weary again by late afternoon. She could not come up with a specific trigger for her illness, but she'd had a milder episode in college after a breakup with her boyfriend that had resolved spontaneously over time. In addition both her mother and paternal grandmother suffered from depression.

She was open to medication and supportive psychotherapy, so I gave her a sample packet of an antidepressant to see how it works, and booked another appointment for her the following week. She kept that appointment but told me she had taken only one dose of the medication. Her father, an internal medicine specialist, was "really upset; he doesn't really trust psychiatrists. He thinks that all you guys do is medicate your patients, especially minority folks, and that psychiatric medications are dangerous. He doesn't want me to see you. He told me to give this more time and return to Wednesday evening bible study."

She gave me permission to call him, so I phoned his office and was put through to his "confidential voice mail." I left a brief message introducing myself and explaining why I was calling. I asked him to return my call so I could answer his questions and explain my treatment plan for his daughter. He didn't. After three days, I tried one more time. This time I actually told the receptionist that my call was personal and requested that she ask the doctor to call me back. He didn't respond to that call either. My patient cancelled her next visit and didn't respond when I phoned her.

This doctor-father's worries were rooted in shameful American history and are not unfounded. Even today, in many top-notch medical centers, there are bold examples of micro-inequities of care for racial and ethnic minority patients. I regret not being able to have a conversation with him about his daughter and, hopefully, reassure him about fair and standard contemporary treatment of depression. I hope his daughter did improve and will perhaps find a psychiatrist who is a better fit for her down the road.

In another instance, Dr. White, a forty-eight-year-old nephrologist, had been my patient for about seven years when he remarried. He was in recovery from alcoholism and was no longer being monitored by his state physician health program. I was also treating him for a longstanding social anxiety disorder, and he had been stable for some time on a low dose of an antidepressant medication that works well for this kind of anxiety disorder.

His new wife, Dr. Stone, was also a physician and a recovering alcoholic whom he'd met at AA. She was really upset about his being on meds. At first he thought she was worried that he would become addicted to the medication even though it was not a habit-forming drug. They talked and talked about how much the medication helped him, but she really wanted him to taper off and stop taking the drug. He refused, and that made her angry. A couple of weeks passed and then his prescription bottle went missing. He asked her if she'd seen it and she said that she had flushed the pills down the toilet. He then asked her to accompany him to his next visit with me, and she agreed. I explained the rationale and argument for the medication, described what Dr. White was like before and how the medication had relieved his anxiety symptoms. I also told her that he had never required a higher dose and that he'd had Cognitive Behavior Therapy in the past, which also helped but did not fully eradicate his panicky feelings in social situations. I explained that I saw his pharmacological treatment as an important feature of relapse prevention, meaning that it reduced the likelihood of his going back to drinking.

She didn't argue with any of this, but asked if I could spend the remainder of the session with her alone. Dr. White was fine with this, and once we were alone, she told me a lot about herself. When she was growing up her mother was addicted to barbiturates prescribed by her psychiatrist, and her efforts to confiscate them were to no avail because the doctor just kept prescribing more and more. Her mother was in and out of psychiatric units, including the one where Dr. Stone went to medical school. She was deeply ashamed of her mother and of her own alcoholism. I suggested that she too could benefit from psychotherapy; she was very open to that idea.

In this instance, I was fortunate enough to meet with my patient's family member who was struggling with stigma, and her openness to working on her own made it possible for her husband to continue his treatment without any further interference from her.

In this chapter I've outlined the many faces of stigma and how stigma can so adversely affect wholesome help seeking and important treatment. But even when stigma is not so present – or has been soothed – there are times when the path to seeking help is not smooth sailing. It's time to discuss how being trained as a physician puts doctors at heightened risk of suicide, the subject of the next chapter.

CHAPTER 7

HOW MEDICAL KNOWLEDGE CAN KILL YOU

Two weeks before he died, Anthony tried to procure [a toxic chemical]...
They told him it was only available in industrial quantities. When a
representative of a scientific supply company in Ohio asked about his
order, he concocted an elaborate lie about using it to clean precious metals:

"All work with this chemical is done under a recirculating chemical fume
hood at a solution concentration of 1g/L [using] this solution I use a face
shield and PVC gloves to protect myself from inadvertent contamination
or spills. Release of HCN from this solution is prevented by the alkaline
pH of the solution".

The rep accepted his explanation but when the order didn't ship as soon as
Anthony had hoped he wrote again to see what was taking so long. His
package arrived a few days later.

From *"My Brother's Life, Unraveled"* by Alex Halperin, mentioned
earlier, writing in *Salon* March 12, 2013.[37]

Medical students have already taken several pre-med courses in chemistry.
In medical school they take even more chemistry as well as courses in

pharmacology. They learn about the uses, effects, modes of action, and potential side effects of drugs that are used to treat diabetes, heart disease, pain, psychiatric conditions, and more. When doing their clerkships or electives in the emergency room, intensive care units, and psychiatric wards, they are exposed to many patients who have tried to kill themselves with many different kinds of over-the-counter and prescribed medications. As they progress through medical school and residency in their specialty they gain both increasing knowledge about and heightened respect for drugs, their uses and their potentially toxic effects.

Along the way they also learn which drugs are particularly lethal in overdose, which ones put someone asleep quickly and rapidly lead to death, and which ones do not cause pain. This knowledge is important but can also be personally risky if and when a physician becomes depressed and despairing and begins to plan a way to kill himself. This may lead to ordering and purchasing medications on line, stockpiling medications that have been prescribed for them, stealing toxic drugs from the hospital, buying drugs on the street, or writing prescriptions using an alias.

Internal medicine and critical care physicians know that injecting potassium chloride or insulin causes a rapid loss of consciousness and death. Anesthesiologists know that barbiturate drugs and fentanyl kill rapidly. Psychiatrists know that tricyclic antidepressants cause deadly arrhythmias when taken in large quantities. Any desperate physician with a life-threatening allergy knows only too well how to expose him or herself and conveniently "forget their EpiPen." Two means of suicide that are becoming more common among medical students and physicians over the past few years are helium inhalation and cyanide poisoning.

Doctors also kill themselves with guns, by hanging, jumping, vehicular crashes, drowning, and more. All of these are considered "lethal means," indicating that the individual is deadly serious about wanting to die and does not want to be rescued and resuscitated. In many instances I've found that my physician patients have also done extensive Internet research. They want to get it right; they want it to be foolproof; they want to die quickly and completely.

Other survivors might determine that it was "not their time" and that their survival has a purpose, such as using their story as a way to prevent another death. One physician who had made elaborate suicide plans and yet survived described her experience this way:

> *I swallowed all the drugs and had a near death experience. I saw my grandmother who died when I was 12, along with other family members. I remember a voice – plus a pure whiteness – saying "It's not your time yet." The voice also stated three principles that I should follow in my life: To make a difference in the world for the better; to earn the admiration of someone or a group; and to be a good man, a good person.*

> *Everything reversed itself. I reentered my body. Then I heard my younger brother trying to wake me up and I thought, "I'm alive, why am I still here?" I still felt that darkness and despair. How could no one notice?*

> *My next and last suicide plan involved driving my car into a wall at a shopping mall. As I raced up the street, I heard the same voice from my last attempt say, "It's not your time." After that, I felt a certain peace.*

> *I continued going for help and over time, started coming out of my despair. In my third year of medical school, I began transitioning from male to female. I went to a psychotherapist who helped me with this. I also learned that 100 percent of transgendered youth are suicidal at one time or another.*

> *I have never been suicidal or attempted suicide again since that time when I was 16 years old. Yet, I make it a point of self-disclosing my suicidality*

with my medical residents. I feel strongly that students look for concrete examples to help them understand and expand their knowledge. The fact that I can resonate with suicidal patients as a psychiatrist and explain the feeling of despair to my residents feels like a gift. My pain can now help others.[38]

In this short chapter, I've added another risk factor that puts **some** doctors at risk, certainly not all. This is important in our understanding of where the thoughts of desperate doctors can lead to. The lack of medical knowledge even figures in the thoughts of the offspring of physicians who struggle with depression and suicidal thoughts. Here are the words of Jeffery Wolk, the grandson of Dr. Maurice Grossberg, who died by suicide in 1939, and whom I mentioned earlier:

"I remember having the thought that Maurie was a lucky man because he was a doctor and as a doctor he knew how to kill himself – and I don't know how. I remember being angry and jealous that Maurie Grossberg knew how to kill himself and I didn't."[39]

CHAPTER 8

DANGEROUS DEFECTS IN HOW PHYSICIANS ARE TREATED AND WHAT CAN BE DONE ABOUT IT

A depressed and suicidal emergency physician described the painful process of trying to find a psychiatrist when she took a position in a new location.

> *I went to my colleagues and got some names of psychiatrists…and I started making phone calls. It was quite the little odyssey. I'd call someone. I'd talk to them for two or three minutes and they'd say well my practice is closed. And I'd say that I'm a new physician in town…and I'm in trouble here, I'm quite depressed and I need some help. Then they'd say "Are you suicidal?" And I wasn't willing to admit to anyone at the time that I was. So I'd say "No, I'm not." and they'd say again "Well I'm really sorry but my practice is closed. I'm afraid you're going to have to find someone else"…So this happened over and over again. And I was in such a bad way. The rejection that I would feel was so extreme…I'd hang up the phone…I would cry for a couple of hours…and not bring myself to make another phone call for days to weeks.*

From *"Physicians Living with Depression"*[40]

Although I interviewed this young physician twenty years ago for this documentary I can still feel what was going on inside me as I listened to her story. I was angry that my profession failed her in her time of need; we did not listen carefully and intuitively to her deep distress and suffering. She didn't express disappointment but how could she not feel that inside? I felt deeply embarrassed that she was treated so dismissively. And I was so relieved that she did not kill herself. An astute resident in psychiatry did reach out to her at work and got her an appointment with a psychiatrist the next day. Her "odyssey" ended there with appropriate and compassionate care. Her gift to the mental health professionals who have looked at this videotape is huge: **never** gauge a complete stranger's degree of suicidality by a simple "no" response to a question over the phone.

Dr. Kay Bauman and Dr. Mark Lupin have both lost a physician loved one to suicide – Dr. Bauman her husband, Jim, and Dr. Lupin his brother, Daniel. Both have published evocative pieces in medical journals examining the ways in which the system of care falls apart when a doctor becomes ill, and calling for change, not just in the mechanism of care delivery but in the hearts and minds of their colleagues and those of us who are entrusted with their care.

When I reviewed their articles[41,42] I noted being struck by the eerie parallels between the two. They describe their loved ones as experiencing almost identical symptoms and struggles: deep depression (triggered by loss and stress), panicky thinking about ruin, suicide attempts before hospitalization, efforts to receive treatment in nearby communities, the stigma of psychiatric illness, worries about loss of their medical license, their exquisite vulnerability to the actions and power of hospital administrations, and their many talents apart from medicine. Both believe that these tragic deaths might have been prevented.

Most people think that, because they are physicians, doctors who become ill have access to the best physicians and get the best treatment that's available. In truth, however, not only do many physicians not get this gold standard of care, but they often do not receive the same level of care (especially mental health care) as members of the general public. Instead, they fall through the cracks, which accounts for an unknown number of doctors dying by suicide each year in the United States.

THE ROLE OF THE PCP

While it's true that many doctors do not have a primary care physician, that's a tale for another time. What I want to focus on here is what can happen when a doctor does have a PCP. Too often even the best treat their doctor patients differently. They may "skip" asking personal health questions such as those having to do with alcohol use, sexual functioning, sexual orientation, extramarital sexual activity, exposure to sexually transmitted diseases, or practicing safe sex, to name just a few. Or, on physical examination, they may omit breast, genital, and rectal exams. In most cases the treating physician thinks he is protecting his patient's privacy or does not want to be viewed as insulting or probing. What happens though is that this initial treatment sets the tone for the relationship going forward so that, if or when the doctor-patient needs to talk about tough subjects - problematic drinking or drug use, stress at home or work, mood swings, thoughts of suicide – he won't do it, because he assumes that these are not the kinds of things one is supposed to share with a PCP.

WHAT ABOUT PSYCHIATRISTS?

Psychiatrists who treat doctor-patients may be nervous or intimidated when treating a fellow physician. Years ago a psychiatrist colleague of mine told me that he really didn't like looking after doctors. When I asked him why, he laughed and said, "I can't get away with my usual bullshit." Although he couched it as a joke, it was a true statement. Translate – you feel exposed when you treat physicians because your patient more or less knows what you're doing. And that's a good thing. For two decades I taught a course with my psychiatrist colleague and friend Dr. Leah Dickstein, professor emerita at the University of Louisville, at the annual spring meeting of the American Psychiatric Association called Treating Medical Students and Physicians. Most of those who took the course were residents or young psychiatrists who wanted to become more comfortable – and adept – at treating their physician colleagues.

Much like PCPs who omit key parts of their examination of doctor patients, psychiatrists who treat physicians may leave out fundamental parts of their inquiry and neglect to ask some important questions. They erroneously assume that because their patient is a doctor, he or she will volunteer what is bothering him. This is especially true when it comes to thoughts of suicide. However, many physicians who are thinking about suicide (or who have attempted suicide in the past) are very private about it. They may feel guilty or embarrassed about thoughts of ending it all. Or they wonder about how the psychiatrist is going to react. Will he not take the admission seriously? Will he overreact and want his patient to go to an emergency room or be admitted to a psychiatric unit? Will he report the doctor to his dean, training director, employer, or state medical licensing board? It is scary enough to be having thoughts of suicide; it is even more frightening to have to worry about the consequences of sharing something so private with your doctor.

"If given the opportunity to treat a fellow physician, psychiatrists should double their compassion and double their skepticism," says one physician who lost his brother, also a physician, to suicide.

Some doctor-patients, even if they are not intending to deceive, may make light of their problems or even try to charm the unsuspecting psychiatrist looking after them. Therefore, psychiatrists who are not very experienced in assessing and treating doctors need to be vigilant and, if they have any doubts, seek a second opinion from a more experienced colleague. This kind of hypervigilance is particularly important when the treating doctor senses a discrepancy between the picture being painted by his patient and the way he looks or seems. The challenge for the treating psychiatrist is to not underdiagnose his patient, who will then not receive the care that could save his life.

Keeping good boundaries is essential when physicians treat physicians. It is pretty straightforward when psychiatrists treat physician-patients. They do not generally accept friends or colleagues as patients because of an inability to be completely objective and to provide unbiased and standard care. But the boundaries are less well-defined and strict with other branches of medicine, say when primary care physicians treat other doctors or obstetricians deliver physician colleagues' babies or pediatricians treat the children of medical friends or associates. Here is an example of a widow who expressed concerns in my interview with her about her late husband's treatment:

"I've done a lot of thinking since Art's death. I'm wondering about all of the factors that can go wrong when a doctor goes to another doctor for help. In my husband's case, one of his doctors was someone who was once his employee. It was only later that this woman became his treating physician but still...I really wonder about a conflict-of-interest...or if not that, a power imbalance. Like too many connections, too close, too much history. It's not really a normal doctor patient relationship with the degree of objectivity or neutrality that I think we all need when we turn over our health care to our physician. I'm not faulting her, I'm not blaming her. In fact, if anyone is responsible it might be my husband because it's possible that he went to her because he already knew her, liked her, respected her.

But she may have let him get away with too much or maybe wasn't firm enough with him, or maybe she let him "manipulate" her. I don't know, it's all speculation, but I'm looking for things we can learn. Losing Art was, and is, so hard. I'm just trying to spare other families of doctors down the road this heartache."

Dr. Gray (pseudonym) lost her physician husband to suicide in 2012

Performing what we call a suicide risk assessment requires knowledge and skill. And there is an art to doing it. It is not just about asking questions or going through a detailed checklist. It is about creating an atmosphere of safety and a trusting relationship. This is especially so when the patient is a physician. In order to be honest, he must feel listened to, respected, and cared for. The psychiatrist, in turn, must believe that he is fully informed and clear about next steps to be taken. And the patient must have confidence in the treating doctor's judgment and treatment plan, whatever that might be.

All of the above is, however, only the beginning. Truly understanding the suicidality of another person is a process that unfolds over time. There are nuances and subtleties. It is not binary – I am suicidal vs I am not suicidal. One thing that I have learned from being a psychiatrist who treats doctors for more than three decades is that, for many depressed physicians, having a suicide plan is very comforting. They take solace in the knowledge that killing themselves is an option to relieve their suffering. As someone who bears witness to these dark states in doctors and is not afraid to venture there with them, I also know that this journey can be restorative and therapeutic. Many of my patients have ended such a session with statements like, "Thank you. Just talking about my private hell, this black hole I've fallen into, has helped a lot. It's kind of weird, but after talking about my suicidal thoughts and plans, I don't feel so suicidal anymore." They are talking about connection – and connection is well known to decrease suicidal acts. And the reason for this is because feelings of isolation, loneliness and alienation bombard and consume suicidal individuals. The vast majority feel a bit better, even more hopeful, when someone extends a hand.

WHAT SHOULD PHYSICIAN-PATIENTS EXPECT FROM TREATING PSYCHIATRISTS?

This is no different than what any person should expect from a psychiatrist they have contacted. But what is not the same is that physician callers often call the psychiatrist directly as opposed to Mr John Doe or Ms Jane Doe who usually have their primary care physician making the referral on their behalf:

- They should expect the psychiatrist to call them back by the end of the working day or certainly within 24 hours. In fact, if there is a tone of urgency in the caller's voice or any hint of acute illness (including desperation or suicidal thinking), the psychiatrist should call back as soon as she gets the message. Even though the caller may be a complete stranger, the psychiatrist might at least be able to suggest an immediate visit to the nearest emergency room or calling 911. Safety is paramount.

- If the situation is not an emergency, the psychiatrist should be prepared to spend a few minutes with the physician caller in order to get a sense of why the doctor is calling and his symptoms. Simply listening attentively and asking a couple of questions not only helps to get a quick understanding of what's going on but conveys a positive message to the doctor – a message of interest and concern.

- When the psychiatrist responds promptly to the physician calling, he is conveying a message of professionalism. A cordial and welcoming voice eases the fear and shame most physicians feel when they make this phone call.

- Ideally, a first appointment should be booked as soon as possible, even if the situation does not seem to be an emergency. If that isn't possible – because of the psychiatrist's busy schedule – and the patient will have to wait two weeks or more, it would be courteous of the psychiatrist to tell the new patient that if there is a cancellation, he will be notified. By doing this, the psychiatrist is essentially saying "I wish I could see you sooner because I know what it's like to wait for help when you're feeling the way you do." It would also be helpful for the psychiatrist to let the new patient know that, "If you're feeling worse over the next couple of weeks and haven't heard from us (me), call back so we can talk again over the phone and you can update me on your condition."

- All new physician patients should expect their psychiatrist to do a thorough biopsychosocial assessment. In other words, the psychiatrist will carefully assess biological contributors to the problem, such as a family history of depression, anxiety, suicide, alcoholism and other substance use disorders; any current medical problem that may be playing a role like diabetes, thyroid illness, heart disease, dementia, etc; any prescribed medications that may have side-effects that can affect one's mental health; the effects of alcohol or other drug use on mental health; any history of head trauma that may be playing a role. Psychological factors include things like childhood abuse or trauma, divorce of parents, bullying, losses, failures, relationship breakups, marital discord, problems with children, problems with training and work, demotions, being fired, being sued, license investigations and more. Social factors are broader cultural factors and may include things like racial and ethnic discrimination, sexism at work, immigration, being a refugee, poverty and severe debt, and stress associated with being LGBT in the training institute or medical workplace. This is a lot to cover but essential nonetheless. And the assessment may be extended over a couple of hours or conducted over two or three standard forty-five- to fifty-minute visits.

- Although the doctor-patient has trained in general medicine and has perhaps some notion of what an anxiety disorder or bipolar illness or obsessive compulsive disorder is, the treating psychiatrist must be careful to explain the diagnosis at a level that is appropriate for the patient. Too much medical jargon (even if the patient is also a psychiatrist) can be confusing and distancing, while using exclusively lay language may be insulting. The psychiatrist should also make sure there is time for the patient to ask questions and for the treating doctor to answer them fully.

- If medication is recommended both the argument for prescribing drugs and the reason for a particular medication need to be explained. Clear directions should be given and possible side-effects described. Interactions with other medications that the doctor-patient may be taking need to be discussed as do use of alcoholic beverages while on psychiatric medications. Once again, this should be a dialogue with the patient being invited to ask any and all questions.

- Psychotherapy should accompany all diagnoses. It should not be an either-or discussion. Research shows that patients with depression respond best to a combination of antidepressants and psychotherapy, not medication alone.

Dr. Mike Shooter, past president of the Royal College of Psychiatrists in England, has spoken about his own history of depression. He was in his mid-20s and had just qualified for medical school when it hit, leading him to the brink of suicide. Here are some quotes from an article in which he expresses the importance of both psychotherapy and medication:

"What I had was the good old fashioned face to face psychotherapy. The talking therapy was a godsend; it was a luxury to be able to explore those awful feelings with someone who is not going to be overwhelmed by them, who is not going to be anxious by them, not made angry by them, and who could understand."

"The pills probably helped biochemically. The pills also helped in that, for me, they represented the fact that this was an illness and it wasn't my fault. I was already feeling guilty – I felt so many people had put themselves out to give me a second chance and I had blown it".[43]

Dr. Shooter believes strongly that this illness and being a patient has helped him be a better doctor.

- Psychotherapy has many forms. Basic supportive psychotherapy is extremely helpful when medication is prescribed and the doctor-patient is waiting for it to begin working and continuing to work until their symptoms are gone or their mood is normal again. But supportive psychotherapy on its own also can be the treatment of choice for many psychiatric conditions. In the early weeks this should be at least weekly, maybe twice per week. Cognitive behavior therapy is another type of psychotherapy that works very well both on its own and with medication (if indicated). It is a participatory type of psychotherapy that has great appeal to doctor-patients who like this kind of approach and who like to work on issues at home between sessions. It doesn't require digging up a lot of tough and painful issues from the past, anathema to some physicians. It works well for anxiety and some mood disorders. Long term psychodynamic psychotherapy is helpful for physician-patients who are psychologically minded and who want to get at the origins of their problem(s) and understand themselves better. This is usually weekly for at least 6 months or longer. There are many other types of psychotherapy that the treating psychiatrist might recommend, some of which are specific to certain diagnoses. Dialectical Behavior Therapy (DBT) for borderline personality problems and Collaborative Assessment and Management of Suicidality (CAMS) for treating suicidal behavior in doctors are two examples. There are many more, including couples' therapy, family therapy and group therapy.

- What about second opinions? All physician-patients should expect their psychiatrist to bring up the subject of getting another opinion if progress is not being made. This may involve traveling to a nearby university setting where sub-specialists in psychiatry tend to work. This person may be a specialist in psychiatric medications (a biological psychiatrist or psychopharmacologist) who is used to treating what is called "treatment resistant depression". Or the psychiatrist may be a specialist in electroconvulsive therapy or vagus nerve stimulation or transcranial magnetic stimulation. Some depressions are very tough to treat and sophisticated treatments may be necessary. What is most important in the face of treatments not really working is not to give up and to know that more expert help is available.

- Physicians who become patients should expect some basic education from their psychiatrist about their illness. One lesson learned from my interviews with the loved ones of doctors who have taken their own lives, is the crying need for education about the mental illnesses that plague physicians. I have heard this from physician loved ones too. One widow told me this: "I don't think my husband really understood what he was living with. Yes, he was a physician and he was being treated for depression and he knew that but I don't think he really understood how much it had taken over his life, consumed him and crushed him. The sad part is that although he called it an illness, he still blamed himself for being that way and not getting better. I'm an oncologist. Severe depression is no different than metastatic cancer, it spreads relentlessly, and invades every facet of your life – your spirits, your self-esteem, your thinking, your work and your family. And most definitely, your soul. In hindsight, my husband's suicide makes so much sense, he saw no way out of the hell he was in."

- They should also expect that their psychiatrist will be interested in educating their family too. A man I interviewed, an attorney and the son of a physician, said "We need to be educated too. I know so much more now about severe addiction since my dad's death. Some is from the internet and some is from what I'm learning in the Adult Children of Alcoholics group I'm attending. Although my dad didn't have a drinking problem, it was cocaine, I now see how out of control he was and the shame of his relapses. I blamed him for a long time. I've forgiven him now. But I still wish he was with us. He would have been a terrific grandfather to my son".

- It is well known that a physician's pride and independence can get in the way when he falls ill. I say this to explain his need to "put his best foot forward" and a tendency to omit essential dimensions of his current symptoms, functioning, habits and past history. Even the most experienced psychiatrist is not able to get the full picture of what's going on and why he's not well at the moment. Physician health specialists like myself are now recommending that treating psychiatrists should – in many cases, not all – tell the doctor-patient that they would like to have a visit (or even a telephone call) with one or more loved ones. This might be a spouse or partner, a parent or parents, a child or children or a sibling depending on the family composition and role of significant others. This will involve discussion, signed consent and rules around confidentiality. The technical term is "collaborative or collateral information". Although doing this is very common in emergency rooms and inpatient psychiatry units, it is less often done in outpatient and private practice settings. And yet the goal is the same – to gather any and all information that might be contributing to the psychiatric illness so that the psychiatrist can implement the best form of treatment. I don't need to highlight how essential this can be when a psychiatrist is treating a very depressed and despairing physician.

- Doctor patients can also expect their psychiatrist to request old records. And in the face of resistance, anticipate that their psychiatrist will push for, if not insist upon, obtaining previous medical records, when the physician has been treated in the past by a different mental health professional at a different time and place. This is an essential requirement of a good standard of care. It obviously involves a signed release from the doctor-patient who may not willingly grant this. The treating psychiatrist should explore this in a fact-finding and empathic manner but should not capitulate to the patient. All doctors have had it drilled into their heads in medical school and residency training about requesting and reviewing the old record. I highlight this because the previous psychiatric records of physicians can yield medically critical information that has not been disclosed to the new psychiatrist. Examples are things like a previous suicide attempt (and the use of a lethal method like a gun, hanging, carbon monoxide or intravenous sedatives), an undisclosed addiction, a bout of mania, an unsubstantiated accusation of unprofessional behavior, a sexual assault and so forth.

Dr. Judy Melinek, a forensic pathologist and co-author with TJ Mitchell of the medical memoir *"Working Stiff: Two Years, 262 Bodies, and the Making of a Medical Examiner"*[44] knows this only too well. Dr. Melinek lost her father Dr. Menachem Melinek, a psychiatrist, to suicide in 1983. He hanged himself 24 hours after being psychiatrically cleared from an emergency room after overdosing on medication. In a telephone interview that I had with Dr. Melinek February 15, 2016 she conveyed, with vigor and passion, the following:

"Mental health professionals who treat doctors need to realize that if you only see the physician, you're only getting their side of the story, what they want you to know or what they're willing to share with you. You must talk with the family members who live with the person, your patient, and have their own particular observations, hunches, ideas and fears. You really have to ask about drug seeking and drug use – and also remember that blood specimens are more accurate for toxic levels than urine specimens. We need to borrow a piece from the early years of the AIDS pandemic and the sign/slogan 'Silence=Death'. This now applies to suicide. The more we perpetuate the silence surrounding suicide the more

survivors suffer after losing a loved one to suicide and the more isolated that suicidal people themselves feel and the more at risk they are for dying of their suicidality."

PHYSICIAN HEALTH SUBSPECIALTY?

Although there is not a subspecialty in physician mental health – like geriatric or child or forensic psychiatry – there is a substantial body of research that continues to grow each year. It is important that psychiatrists who treat physicians keep abreast of this research. Most general and specialist medical journals publish scientific articles on physician burnout and depression or addiction in doctors. Some offer blogs that cover this material. Medical institutions invite psychiatrists and addiction specialists to present grand rounds for continuing medical education. Books and DVDs are available. There is a biennial international conference on physician health sponsored by the American, Canadian and British Medical Associations that is open to all psychiatrists to enhance their knowledge of physician health and enhance their confidence in treating doctors. These efforts are all directed toward ensuring that when doctors get ill they get good care.

THE ROLE OF STATE PHYSICIAN HEALTH PROGRAMS

Almost every state has a program set up to serve ailing doctors. Initially established in the 1970s to assist with the early diagnosis and treatment of alcohol and other drug problems, these programs have now expanded their outreach to include all kinds of stress-related problems including burnout, depression, bipolar illness, PTSD, eating disorders, and more. They work at arm's length from the medical licensing boards to make sure that physicians get treatment - not punishment for being ill. They do not report physicians

119

to licensing authorities unless the doctor has not cooperated with treatment and there is evidence that she may be impaired – in other words, not able, because of illness, to provide safe and competent care to her patients.

One type of complaint that has arisen about some of these programs is that they are best equipped to help doctors with alcoholism and drug addictions to the exclusion of non-chemical mental problems. It is believed that they use the time-honored twelve-step recovery model for physicians with alcohol and other drug problems (which is appropriate) and do not include much-needed general psychiatric assessment and treatment (which is not appropriate). One reason may be that they are not adequately funded or staffed with people who have that kind of expertise. For a suicidal doctor, however, this could be quite dangerous, because the depth or degree of his potential to harm himself may be missed or normalized or minimized. There is no problem if those who run the program accept the fact that they are not equipped to offer this kind of treatment and refer the doctor to the correct individual or facility. But it is problematic if they do not realize the degree to which the physician is at risk.

Drs. Karen and Robert Miday, whom I interviewed for this book, lost their son Greg to suicide in 2012. He was twenty-nine years old. "Greg was exceptional," they told me. "Brilliant. He had a letter to the editor published in the *New York Times* when he was in college. He was an art history major. He was very musical. All this before medical school and residency. He really didn't meet the criteria for depression (meaning Major Depressive Disorder). Later we wondered about subsyndromal depression (another technical diagnostic term for a type of depression) – or bipolar II illness (a milder form of bipolar or manic-depressive illness). We think he panicked; he had a history of anxiety and panic. He also suffered from substance dependence. But despite all the treatment, he never really accepted it. He admitted that he didn't think he was in full recovery. He was about to start his fellowship. His Caduceus group had ended. He was afraid he'd lose his medical license. The Physician Health Programs vary a lot across the country. In Greg's case there was no psychiatric consultation, no notion of concurrent co-morbidities, and no internal review of any conflicts of interest. There need to be better guidelines nationally, a model program needs to be mandated. We think that Greg died because of shame."

To my knowledge, the Federation of State Physician Health Programs (the national body) is very aware of this problem and is vigorously working on ways to support such programs and bring them up to the gold standard for early identification, comprehensive assessment, broad-based treatment, and acceptable monitoring of doctors under their watch.

At the end of the day, all psychiatrists who treat physicians need to use the same skill sets to diagnose and treat them as they use with their non-physician patients. They must not let them elude the care that is necessary to get well. And stay well. Many physicians when they become ill feel like they are a burden or that they are taking up too much of the psychiatrist's time. Or that they are not sick enough. If I was given a dollar for every doctor patient of mine who has said to me "Shouldn't you be looking after homeless schizophrenics?" I would be a very rich man indeed. Some doctors just don't feel worthy of being cared for. Others abhor dependency in themselves and cannot accept that psychiatric illnesses make you feel dependent on others. Having to rely on your psychiatrist when you're severely depressed is normal. Doctors just need to be reassured that this is temporary and soon they will be feeling and functioning well again. And they may need to be told that this is no different than being under the watchful vigilance of your oncologist if you're being followed for cancer or your cardiologist after a heart attack.

PART THREE

THE GOOD NEWS: SUICIDE CAN BE PREVENTED

CHAPTER 9

RESTORING HUMANITY IN OUR MEDICAL SCHOOLS AND RESIDENCY PROGRAMS

To ensure safe passage through medical school, students need to feel respected, valued and cared for – in effect, like the doctors of tomorrow. Teaching the basics of medicine and graduating competent physicians is not enough. At the root of so much burnout in today's medical students is a sense of powerlessness, alienation and fatigue.

There has been a sea change in medical education over the past decade or more. One such change was the creation of the Gold Humanism Honor Society, started in 2001 by the Arnold P Gold Foundation in hopes that the values of humanism and professionalism would be recognized in individuals who demonstrate excellence in clinical care, leadership, compassion, and dedication to service. Dr. Gold is a pediatric neurologist at Columbia University College of Physicians and Surgeons. He and his wife Dr. Sandra Gold formed the Foundation in 1988. One offshoot of this are mandatory courses in narrative medicine, which bring students together with a leader or facilitator to talk about the feelings they have the first time they have to face a particularly difficult situation such as dissecting a human body, witnessing or assisting at a cardiac arrest and resuscitation, breaking bad news to a patient about her diagnosis, losing a patient to death, seeing a battered baby in pediatrics or a stillborn in obstetrics, listening to the story of a rape victim in the ER, seeing patients with massive injuries, or visiting an intensive care unit. In these sessions, it is okay to cry, to be frightened, to be angry, to be embarrassed. Much is normalized and much is learned about psychological growth and enhanced empathy through these rites of passage.

Deans, associate, and assistant deans increasingly understand the complexity of their students' lives. They are educated in diversity and cultural competence. They ensure that counseling is available for students encountering problems that range from adjustment to medical school to learning disabilities to psychological and psychiatric illnesses.

Learning assistance centers are the norm on campus as are general medical and psychiatric health services. Confidentiality is key and students' clinical records are completely separate from their academic file.

Sessions on wellness, how to recognize burnout, depression, and suicidal signs in oneself or classmates, mindfulness based meditation, yoga, access to a gym and more are also in place.

Some medical schools have an ombudsman (or woman) to investigate non-academic stresses such as feeling abused by a senior student, resident, or faculty member or being subjected to unprofessional behavior by someone in authority or another health professional. Some schools have a buddy system, big brother/little brother or big sister/little sister pairings and peer counseling. Others have a 24-hour hotline that acts as a crisis center for medical students and resident physicians who are in acute emotional distress.

And yet, this is not enough. As much as these systemic changes in our medical schools are helping the doctors of tomorrow – and they indeed are – an unknown number of medical students in the United States are still taking their own lives each year.

Chapter 9: Restoring Humanity in Our Medical Schools and Residency Programs

I reached out to Rhonda Elkins, who started a blog and wrote a book after her daughter, Kaitlyn, a medical student, took her own life in 2013.[45] Rhonda responded to my email by saying how important it was to her to educate people about, as she put it, "hidden depression in the highly achieving." She said that her mind would not rest "until this problem is brought more to the forefront. No one knows brilliant people can go around wanting to die. They need to know, parents need to know, and the young people need to know that they are not the only one so they will actually seek help."

I wish I'd had the opportunity to speak with Rhonda, but, as she told me in her email, she too had suffered from depression, and sadly, she took her own life four months later. I believe it is essential that her message to students, their parents, their peers, deans, and medical school faculty members not be forgotten: high achieving students living with suicidal depression may conceal their condition from everyone around them, and, because of that, they do not receive the life-saving treatment that is available and that they deserve.

WHAT CAN BE DONE?

All physicians learn basic psychiatry in medical school. The intent is to educate all medical students about the most common mental illnesses that they may see in their patients after graduation. Most medical students spend 4-6 weeks on an inpatient unit of a teaching hospital where they observe (and often participate in) the treatment of patients with schizophrenia, bipolar illness, severe depression and substance use disorders (alcohol and other drug use). Students who are considering primary care and psychiatry usually sign up for one or two additional months gaining experience in consultation or outpatient settings, geriatrics, child and adolescent psychiatry and so forth. But otherwise this is their only exposure to psychiatric illness. And their patients are usually the most severely affected too. They are not going to be exposed to patients who are much like themselves – high functioning, goal oriented and disciplined. What they learn in school is a diagnostic and skill set to help others. Most would not look inward and see that this information might help them someday.

It seems to me that general education of our medical students about psychiatric illnesses, especially depression, falls short. Knowing what to look for in yourself and your peers will help a lot of students to identify what might be happening and to reach out for assistance. Especially if we are increasingly successful at reducing the stigma attached to accepting treatment. But for the cohort of students who may pay lip service to these offerings or – in all fairness – are extremely private or categorically refuse to see a therapist, something different is needed.

Ideally they would observe a live interview (conducted by a mental health professional) with a medical student or young physician who has been deeply depressed and suicidal. Someone who recognized that he or she was ill but did not seek care. Someone who speaks about why he didn't think he needed help or who dismissed the potential value of psychiatric assistance, and who then discusses the worsening of his condition and its effect on his school work, his ability to concentrate and retain what he was studying. His confidence and self-esteem dropped and his suicidal thinking became more frequent, intense, and alternatingly terrifying and comforting. He then describes his decision to die and what he did to harm himself. It was at that time that psychiatric treatment began. And now he can report what that entailed and how he began to feel better.

Of course, it is highly unlikely that any medical school would have access to anyone so open to speaking about his suicidal depression and its treatment. What would be second best is using a "standardized patient," that is, an actor who plays the part of the young physician with this story. He might also be trained to answer questions posed by students in the audience. But what would be most important is how well trained the actor is and how carefully scripted the story is. Having a psychiatric consultant who is clinically experienced in treating real live physician patients is key. Otherwise, he will not be convincing and might even reinforce the students' denial that this could ever happen to them or to a medical peer.

What could also be effective is a brief seminar during which students watch a short DVD or film of a medical student or doctor telling her story, followed by discussion with an experienced psychiatrist who can field their questions. But once again, this has to be convincing and there needs to be buy-in by the students. The doctor patient needs to be someone with whom they can identify and make an empathic connection. The documentary part needs to be brief and tightly edited in order to hold their attention. Most important, given the cultural mosaic of our medical schools today, the more diverse in gender and ethnicity the live doctors, videotaped doctors, or standardized patients the better.

WHAT ABOUT RESIDENTS?

"It is with a heavy heart that I write this…."

The unbearable has happened at the University of Kentucky. Last Friday we discovered that one of our residents was tragically taken from us. It appears that the resident took their own life in response to acute grief over a moribund family member.

This is a catastrophic loss for our program and for his family and friends. While I am immensely embarrassed that I lost a resident "on my watch" and guilty that I didn't see this coming, this needs to be said. Honestly, I have struggled on whether I should write this email at all. I make this information public in order to shine a bright light on a problem that often lurks in the dark. Suicide, and specifically suicide in our trainees, is a significant risk and we are at higher risk than the general public. In order to face this issue, we must acknowledge its existence. We must "speak its name". We must learn about it and talk about it.

These are the words of Dr. Chris Doty from an email that he sent to his colleagues in Emergency Medicine in January 2016. He is program director at the University of Kentucky-Chandler Medical Center in Lexington. I spoke with him in June 2016 to obtain his permission to write a piece about his response to this tragedy and his taking action.[46] I also thanked him for speaking out and working with the Resilience Committee of the Council of Emergency Medicine Residency Directors and the Wellness Committee of the American Academy of Emergency Medicine in their efforts to prevent further suicides in trainees.

The death of the two interns in New York City that I mentioned earlier in this book also has had a galvanizing effect on many training programs across the country. But most significantly the Accreditation Council for Graduate Medical Education (ACGME) has unreservedly stepped up to the plate to make the health and safe harbor of their trainees their number one priority. They have hosted two very successful symposia in 2015 and 2016 with 150 or so attendees from medical centers far and wide. This is a diverse group of physicians and other health professionals, researchers, designated institutional officials, residents, training directors, deans of post-graduate education, department chairs and health care executives who are deeply committed to study and investigate training issues and milestones, what is working and what isn't, actively learning from each other and preparing the initial stages of a national response. There are several working committees and dedicated resources to actualize the goal of ensuring good health and preventing suicide in today's residents.

Some of the early suggestions and recommendations are: using social media apps for aborting suicidal thinking in residents via cognitive behavioral techniques; 24 hour hot lines for residents in crisis; ensuring privacy and confidentiality in all personal communications (with the exception of immediate intervention for dangerous suicidal behavior); dealing immediately with teachers who are abusive, shaming and threatening; continuing review of the number of expected duty hours and rest time and on-call frequency; burnout prevention strategies in the form of a toolkit available to trainees and their training directors; mental health professional availability to residents in the evening and weekends when they can attend sessions; free (or affordable) care; fatigue reduction strategies; wholesome meals, exercise equipment and on-site day care; comprehensive disability insurance without pre-existing condition exemptions; ensuring that all states have well-staffed and multi-disciplinary professionals serving on their physician health committees; working with the Federation of State Medical Boards to ensure that license application questions ask only about impairing conditions and do not violate the Americans with Disability Act.

At the end of the day it is not enough to simply give a tightly packed day of orientation to our incoming residents with 15-20 minutes crammed in about how to take care of yourself. Lessons have been learned from tragedies and it is time for every resident to expect that he is in good hands in their respective programs. They deserve to graduate four or five years later with not only first rate medical credentials but first rate health too.

A VERY NICE STORY

It helps tremendously when doctors 'go public' with their own stories. Here's an example of a brief piece written by a physician and published in the Louisville Kentucky Courier-Journal under the by-line Contemplating 'epidemic of physician suicide':

A chaotic world full (sic) contrasted with angst and wonder can be a hard pill to swallow for many of us. Too often we lose people we think are invincible or naively thought that they were too strong to break. It's as if certain professions afford a false sense of security that abates when reality materializes.

How often do we ask ourselves who protects the protector? I have been to the doctor with feelings of helplessness and loneliness. I have felt so bad at times that it was a struggle to get out of bed. Depression can be paralyzing and despair can mask itself as a useful companion. But I found hope in the fact that I could go to my physician and have a voice that was listened to. A physician with a set of ears that empathizes and a heart that cares. A physician that would help me.

But what if this person was gone?

I look in the mirror and ask myself that question over and over on an almost daily basis. What if I were gone? Just another physician lost to an epidemic of physician suicide. When will that stop in this world — I want to know.

Curtis Cary, MD[47]

I called Dr. Cary to thank him for sharing his story. I was happy and gratified to hear that several people had emailed him, that they thought he was brave. Most important, others called to offer him support and to check in on him. Half were health professionals and others were lay readers, simply offering to help in any way they might.

THE VALUE OF MEMORIAL LECTURES

A number of medical colleges, organizations, and communities have established a practice of holding memorial lectures after the death by suicide of one of their own. I have been invited to give a number of these talks, and I believe that they serve several important functions. They pay homage to a local student, resident and the work he or she has done in his particular field. They educate members of the audience on the subject of mental illness and the causes of suicide. And probably most importantly, they provide busy medical students and physicians with a reason to pause and reflect.

In 1999 I was invited to give the 7th annual Byron Griffith memorial lecture, established in honor of a student at Tulane University Medical School who died by suicide in 1988. There was a nice turnout and many medical students attended. I can't remember the name of the man who thanked me for coming, but I do remember something he said to me quietly after the talk. He felt bad that there was only a handful of faculty in the room. He believed that their presence would have delivered a powerful message to the students about the importance of memory and paying respect to trainees, the doctors and colleagues of tomorrow. He worried that their absence would demean the significance of those who have fallen. Powerful sentiments. And something for all of us to think about.

CHAPTER 10

REVITALIZING THE
PRACTICE OF MEDICINE

"Healers are attracted to the profession to be a helper, not a helpee. They haven't been given permission to ask for help, they have no experience in asking for help. Someone needs to tell us 'it's ok to get help'. Then you get into medical school, you shut yourself down to get the job done, it's good for administration but not for our health. My self-disclosure is that I have been suicidal, I have felt suicidal. It's important to be authentic. And I recommend transparency, a forced restructuring of our medical system. I dated a man in medical school for 3 years, he died years later by an overdose of methadone. Men don't like to ask for help, even for driving directions, so they can't ask for help as a physician either. Doctors don't know how to grieve, medicine has shut them down, and this is why medical conferences are like funerals. Doctors are dying from despair. My suicidal thoughts were occupationally induced. How could I seek help from a profession that had wounded me? I was determined to get help from someone out of my profession. As a medical profession, we need to grieve collectively. This is a systems issue. There is a collective wound that is best healed by a collective healing."

Excerpts from a telephone interview with Dr. Pamela Wible January 22, 2015. She is a family physician in Eugene OR and writes a blog and offers physician well-being retreats. She is the author of *"Physician Suicide Letters Answered"*[48]

Although work frustration and dissatisfaction are only a part of the many reasons why a doctor decides to kill himself, making changes in how medicine is conducted today will surely raise morale and increase reward. In some cases those changes could save a life. Today's physicians need to recapture the feelings of what drew them to medicine in the first place. Not only they, but their patients, students, and families will benefit.

What doctors can do on their own

First of all, it is essential that physicians monitor themselves for signs of burn out, excessive use of drugs or alcohol, depression, and even family problems.

We all face challenges and obstacles in our professional and private lives. Therefore, doctors - as much if not more so than anyone else – must take care of themselves as they navigate through the often rough waters of medical life.

Those who have just completed medical training and are starting their first job need to understand that this is a time of transition. They will no longer be under regular surveillance but neither will they be receiving regular validation of their work. This can be extremely liberating, but also isolating. Particularly in situations where colleagues don't necessarily interact on a regular basis, it is important to make whatever effort is necessary to stay in touch with peers.

All doctors, but particularly those starting out, need to be mindful of the number of hours they are working. Overwork can lead to burnout down the road, but even before that it can cause an erosion of intimacy and function within the family unit. Especially in the early years, physicians may still be seeking that pat on the back they were used to receiving as perfectionists and accept the fact that they cannot please everyone all the time. Professionally, they will always have angry and disgruntled patients. Personally, spouses and children may be upset when a professional emergency takes time away from the family.

It is important for doctors to feel that they are in charge of their lives. Sometimes it can seem as if the demands of patients, colleagues, department heads, or the institution itself are driving the bus. When that happens the physician may feel powerless and put upon, stressed and discontent. Doctors need to have a sense of "personal agency" and be mindful of how they are managing stress. If it is by drinking too much, self-medicating with drug samples, or behaving badly in public, it's time to do something about it and reach out for help – which is, in fact, a way to stay in charge.

AND DON'T FORGET THE BIG PICTURE

*"My husband Jeff died by his own hand – literally, by injection of a painkiller – quite a few years ago. He had never been depressed before but his father had bipolar illness and both of them lived with a lot of shame and stigma about this. Jeff was stressed and acting kind of bizarrely before he died. He did not seek any treatment. For my husband, medicine was kind of a calling, a legacy, and he came from a family of doctors. I am different. I think it is really important for doctors to know that **medicine is really just a job**, the world will go on without us. I think this would take a lot of pressure off all of us if we accepted this belief."*

Telephone interview with Dr. Stanhope (pseudonym) on February 23, 2015 about the loss of her husband to suicide.

WHAT IS CHANGING IN THE WORLD OF MEDICINE

In chapter 5 I described burnout and how big a problem it's become in today's physicians. Here's how to change that. Many medical centers are scheduling grand rounds on the topic of burnout, and most medical (and specialty) associations have sessions on the subject at their annual meetings. Many physicians come away from these events feeling less cynical and more hopeful. They increasingly realize that they have a voice in this struggle and that they can vote for those candidates running for elected office in their medical associations who listen and who will carry their grievances to key stakeholders – legislative bodies, malpractice insurers, medical licensing authorities, hospital credentialing groups, and any other national bodies who have a say in what's happening in the everyday practice of medicine. For too long physicians have sacrificed their own health and that of their families to serve their patients. And not complain. But the reality of ailing doctors and doctors killing themselves is increasingly impossible to ignore.

Although there is much geographical and specialty variation, fewer physicians are in private practice, and if they are, these are group practices. Solo practitioners are rare today for many reasons. More physicians, especially younger doctors, prefer salaried positions with regular hours and predictable earnings and benefits built into their contracts. This model addresses the importance of having balance in one's life and ideally should provide ample time for personal and family responsibilities, which, in turn, should help to protect against burnout.

Balint groups are also making a comeback in America. Started in the UK in 1969 by Enid and Michael Balint, they are comprised of a small group of physicians coming together on a regular basis to discuss patients. The American Balint Society was formed in 1990 to provide support to physicians and improve the medical care of patients. What is central is the emphasis on physicians trusting one another, frank disclosure and confidentiality. This type of collegiality helps to guard against the alienation and isolation felt by many practicing physicians today.

All in all, physicians are beginning to feel better about their every day work and adapting to many of the changes in the modern medical workplace. First person accounts of doctors rekindling joy in their practices are popping up in our medical journals and blogs. They talk about an increase in assertiveness and self-regard, and to use a contemporary expression, many have found their "voices". They have a much greater sense of personal happiness and fulfillment. They can say with pride that they are part of the movement to return joy to the practice of medicine.

ENLISTING SURVIVORS: SAVING LIVES WITH THEIR STORIES

There are many individuals who have been affected by the death of a physician to suicide who want to get involved in change. They want to share their stories with the wish to help others who are facing what they've been living with. Or they want to save a life, to prevent another doctor from dying by their own hand. Or they want to impart lessons they've learned that inform other health professionals who treat doctors, educators who train doctors, fellow health professionals who work with doctors and anyone who has a physician as a friend or family member. Here are some of their stories:

VIRGINIA LEARY-MAJDA

"John had a twin brother with depression and he warned me that he might be at risk. I was prepared but at the services I was overwhelmed by the shock in others. So many doctors asked 'how did I miss it?'. He died on a

Monday, he was at Tumor Board the Thursday before, he didn't miss a beat. The classic profile was not him. Suicide happens to your golden boys too. I was told he had 'treatment resistant depression' when he was hospitalized the second time. It was compared to cancer that is not responding to chemotherapy. He was on a huge cocktail of medications. He was open with me about being suicidal. He wanted people to know the truth. Neither John nor his psychiatrist wanted him to practice medicine unless he was safe. He had a strong motivation to live. He wanted his patients to know the truth too. I gave them my contact information after he died. Several called to give me their condolences and they mentioned how much he understood them. I was very touched. I've had a hard time with people presuming that I should be angry or ashamed. But I don't. I tell people that my husband was trying to hold on as long as he could. I witnessed his disease. This has to take priority. Patients have to be respected and treated with compassion. I lost my personal physician, a gynecologist to suicide. I knew the truth and so did John but it wasn't talked about. There was a giant elephant in the room. I was heartsick that I couldn't ask 'What happened to my doctor?' I knew that he wouldn't just leave me."

Ms Leary-Majda lost her husband John, a radiation oncologist, to suicide May 28, 2007. The John A Majda, MD Memorial Fund at the UCSD School of Medicine was established within a few weeks of his death.[49] It is her hope that her efforts and that of Dr. Sid Zisook and his committee will lead to a greater understanding of the disease that took his life and prevent others from losing theirs. She spoke at UCSD Psychiatry Grand Rounds in July 2014 as part of a panel "Coping with Suicide: Personal Narratives". What follows is a paragraph that I have retrieved from her annual letter to Friends of the Fund. It captures some of the essence of this wonderful woman:

When it was time for my talk, I left my notes behind and stepped away from the podium. I stood in front of all these physicians and spoke from the heart. Using the looks in their eyes and their reactions as my only guide, I shared my memories. I revealed as much as possible. I did not hold back. I told them what I felt they needed to hear and what I needed to say. John battled a horrific disease that robbed him of everything he loved. Suicide was not his choice. It was the outcome of his disease. Depression is not an attitude. The depressed are not weak or flawed. Before we can help the mentally ill, we need to understand more about mental illness. We need to eradicate the stigma. We need to examine how we feel about the depressed and those lost to suicide. We need to support and understand those who live with the depressed or have lost someone they love to suicide. We need to remove the obstacles to treatment.

DR. LEV GERTSIK (TREATING PSYCHIATRIST OF DR. JOHN MAJDA)

"There were two periods, before and after John's death. When I saw him in consultation, he was Stage 4 (like in a cancer rating), a ticking bomb. I knew he was at high risk. We worked together for four years. He wanted to be my friend more than my patient. I didn't cross any boundaries but I realize now that I would set limits more firmly with my other patients. He killed himself when I was out of the country. So many psychiatrists fear the medical legal consequences of suicide of their patient. This is so different than oncologists. They lose patients and aren't (usually) sued for the death, are they? What is missing is that we don't have stages of severity like for other medical diseases — cancer, diabetes, congestive heart failure, hypertension.

I called John's wife when I got home from my vacation. She was so appreciative. That's the finest praise I've ever received. We don't need to be ashamed. John's death has changed my approach. His death liberated me. I've very aggressive with suicidal people. I'm not warm and fuzzy. So in a way, John has allowed me this style – and I've helped suicidal people since his death with this approach."

Excerpts from my interview with Dr. Gertsik July 2, 2015.

He was also kind enough to send me a paper that he presented at psychiatry grand rounds at UC San Diego and Cedars Sinai Medical Center in Los Angeles. Copied below are some very sage words that address how John did not have the support of his peers. He felt isolated and lived with constant fear of being discovered, humiliated and pushed away:

I promised John's wife to raise this issue today. Physicians in many respects are a privileged class in this country. At the same time, we are subject to extremely high professional and health standards and scrutiny. For physicians with mental illness, those who are not chronically impaired, and their caretakers this provides very limited space to operate to preserve dignity and opportunity to practice. People, who are charged with assuring the standards and safety of practice, do not usually know the physician in question well or at all, and they are much more likely to act safe rather than fair. Collegial support in situations like that may prove to be absolutely invaluable and lifesaving. Practice of medicine, unfortunately - and John's case is evidence to that - is often a solitary existence not supported by a professional group in any personally meaningful way. I want to finish today by pleading to you to consider that and to extend a supporting hand to your peer in need should an opportunity to do so present itself.

ELSIE AND JERRY WEYRAUCH

"Our daughter was born on December 22, 1952 and died on June 17, 1987. She was board certified in internal medicine and rheumatology. It was 7:15 on a Tuesday evening, the Chicago police called and said 'we're looking for her husband – she just hanged herself'. That is how we found out. It is now 28 years later and I recommend to all people, please be empathic when conveying sad news, be compassionate and careful. It took us several years to recover. I (Elsie) still struggle with 'what did I do wrong?'. She was brilliant. She never had a B in her life. After her death, her husband told us that she had unipolar depression. Another recommendation we have is this: be careful of smart people, they can fool you. She was too intelligent for her own good. She hid the depression from us. She was 34 when she ended her life, she was an academic physician, she didn't have other things in her life besides medicine. She was a sensitive woman. I (Elsie) worry about women doctors in academia, it can be hard on women. Her death is still so fresh even after 28 years. You never really get over it. It was so sudden. We called her psychiatrist after she died. He never called us back. Was he afraid of a lawsuit? All we wanted were some answers."

Excerpts from my interview with the Weyrauchs on April 17, 2015. They are the parents of Terri Ann Weyrauch, MD

ROBIN PFISTER

"It was such a shock. We had had a normal weekend. He went off to do urgent care on Sunday from 9am-12noon. He was usually home by 1pm but he called my son and said he'd be home about 4pm. By 5:15 or so he still wasn't home. He was not at the hospital, I called the police, I called his office partner, went to the office. He left all of his ID there. And a

letter to the boys and me that he had committed suicide. He hung himself in the chapel of the hospital. It was a crime scene, there was no ID. I had no idea. No one saw anything. He was such a good doctor, he was so good with kids. But he had trouble passing the boards. Blue Cross was not happy that he wasn't board certified. A lot came out in the letter to us. He admitted that he hadn't been telling us the truth – about some of the rules of the clinic re employability, about drinking ('I never saw his drinking'), that he had been depressed for a long time and taking medication. One of his partners was treating him. This is such a small community and there was a possibility of seeing a psychiatrist but there's that stigma, that is so big in doctors. Also in the letter he wrote 'you and the boys deserve better, I love you all so much'.

I refer to this as trauma. I was afraid to ask for help at first. My therapist takes me in a different direction about treating me for PTSD. I keep seeing the image of pulling the sheet away and identifying his body. I was told you need to tell the kids the truth. If you don't they will find out. I am so committed to helping others. I want to help in any way that I can."

Excerpts from my telephone interview on October 15, 2015. She is the widow of pediatrician Dr. Glen Pfister who died by suicide October 19, 2014.

DR. WILSON (PSEUDONYM)

"Since Carla's death, I've thought very deeply about her – and our work together. I wonder how much she kept from me, how much she didn't share. She was in recovery and being monitored – and although I didn't have to file any reports to the physician health program, I wonder if that inhibited her from being fully truthful with me. Just the process of

oversight, I wonder how much that might work against doctors being completely forthcoming with their therapists. And putting your best foot forward, how much does that play a role when doctors go for help? I learned a lot after her death that she had never shared with me. I wish I had grilled her more. Losing a patient to suicide is like a psychic bomb. It's very traumatic – you feel betrayed, you're angry, you feel so guilty and very ashamed. It's very haunting. I've become a suicide hawk. Recommendations? Self-preservation must come first, we're human beings, we're vulnerable too, like our doctor-patients. We have to recognize and pay attention to our own needs, and find a safe place to talk about ourselves. We need to be humanistic – be open, go there, that can be very moving. Most important, we have to help the survivors. We need to connect to the family, to offer our assistance."

Telephone interview with Dr. Wilson about the loss of his patient, a 28 year old resident in ophthalmology.

Dr. Glen Gabbard

"The first time that I saw her I had a sinking feeling…because she told me she didn't have one good memory of her childhood…and I probed a little bit to see if she could come up with something…and she couldn't…and I just had this sense of blackness about her."

Dr. Gabbard mentions that later in his treatment of the patient, she died of a "Desipramine overdose". He then received a call from the patient's internist that he was prescribing Desipramine as well.

"So I started getting angry. I felt betrayed..she was concealing things from me…she was deceptive…then her friend read her suicide note that said

'Dr. Gabbard was great but he just wasn't enough'...I was moved in some ways but also felt what could I have done that was enough?"

Quotes taken from the DVD *"Collateral Damages: The Impact of Patient Suicide on the Psychiatrist".*

In this teaching film, Dr. Gabbard describes his thoughts and feelings about a young woman physician he was treating who took her own life.[50] This film, which includes the experiences of other psychiatrists, is used in many psychiatry training programs across the United States to help residents prepare for and respond to losing a patient under their care to suicide.

The next two stories are from young physicians who are facing the loss of a physician colleague (Dr. Middleton) and a physician friend and roommate (Dr. Billings, a pseudonym). Both are committed to speaking openly about their loss and getting involved in continuing medical education efforts to make the medical training site and workplace a safe and healthy setting for the next generation of doctors.

DR. JENNIFER MIDDLETON

"Today I learned that you died and nothing will ever be the same again. I refused to believe the words I heard, that you committed suicide. Only terribly depressed people kill themselves. You weren't terribly depressed...but then I learned that, yes, secretly you had been. How could I not know, not realize?"[51]

DR. BILLINGS (PSEUDONYM)

"I saw him briefly when he dropped something off back at the apartment. This was the last time I saw him. He looked at me and shook my hand. He said something, a common use of words, he looked me in the eye. Later

in the afternoon I got a text message from a friend of his friend about his death. I was shell-shocked, thank god my friend was with me. I stayed with him and his girlfriend for about a week or so. This hurts so much. I've repeated to myself 'what were you thinking Todd?'. I'm so fortunate to have started therapy and I have very strong supports in my life."

Fragments of a telephone interview with Dr. Billings about losing his room-mate, another physician, to suicide.

This final story represents the heartache of a man in the arts whose partner thwarted all of his overtures to go for help.

MR TOMLINSON (PSEUDONYM)

"My partner and I were together for 17 years. He told me after several months that he had tried to kill himself in medical school. But he was fine then and for a long time until AIDS hit. He was a ground zero doctor. He came home crying almost every night 'my patients have so much I can't fix'. Then our friends got sick and died. He withdrew and pushed me away. He swallowed Tylenol pills and used booze to cope. I watched him slowly die. There was no way he'd go for help. I pleaded with him. He just wanted to die."

Excerpts from a telephone interview July 14, 2016 with Mr Tomlinson who lost his partner to suicide in the 1990s.

In an email to me after we spoke he wrote this:

Thank you again for giving me this opportunity to tell my story. Even with the pain, it brought great solace. And, I'm so very grateful that you are telling a story that is long overdue in the medical world.

I salute all of these fine individuals. What they share with others is serious and sad, but not depressing. Their stories are full of hope and go the distance in our efforts to revitalize the practice of medicine. Their courage and genuineness touch people's hearts and help many of those individuals to drop facades and face painful truths and realities. It is this process that shifts so much of today's medicine from the frenzied technological, impersonal or corporate atmosphere it has become back to the humanistic, authentic and communal milieu where it belongs.

CHAPTER 11

EDUCATING PHYSICIANS AND THEIR LOVED ONES

"I don't want other people to go through what I've been through. I know so much more now than I did before Gus got sick…and before he died. We, in the medical profession, need to learn more about this, about depression. We got to talk about it more".

The words of Peggy Watanabe, MD, who lost her husband Dr. August Watanabe to suicide.

"There needs to be more education of families. My father was suffering from a derangement of a body organ. That's what killed him. There needs to be greater recognition that depression is a disease with physiological elements. This knowledge will help the broader society…and physicians themselves as they approach their depressed patients."

The words of Frank Watanabe who lost his father Dr. August Watanabe to suicide.

My doctor-patients have taught me an enormous amount about the pressing need for more education – what we call continuing medical education – concerning the illnesses for which physicians are most at risk.

CHAPTER 11: EDUCATING PHYSICIANS AND THEIR LOVED ONES

We need more information made available for doctors who are worried about their own mental health or that of a colleague. They should be able to go online and read about the basic symptoms and signs of depression, obsessive-compulsive disorder, panic disorder and alcohol abuse. This information is available already on the internet for anyone and this can be very helpful for doctors to study. There is also more specific information available for physician readers on the websites of state physician health programs and the American Medical Association but doctors don't necessarily know that. Social media can assist with this so that all doctors know where to turn when or if they need to.

We psychiatrists, in particular, need to step up to the plate and do our part to educate our physician brothers and sisters. You don't have to be a specialist in physician health to teach the basics. But *how* we convey this information is as important as the information itself. Instead of saying, "Here is what to look for in a patient with depression......" Rather we should be saying something like, "Should you be wondering about your own health and functioning, here is what to watch for...And if your symptoms don't go away in two weeks or are rapidly worsening, call your primary care doctor or a psychiatrist." Teaching with a positive spin is absolutely essential.

Psychiatrists who have hospital privileges or who are affiliated with a medical school can also get key messages about wellness out there by forming or serving on the institution's wellness committee. This might include education days, grand rounds, seminars and in-service teaching to small or large groups of one's fellow physicians. By inviting guest speakers who are experts in physician health much information can be conveyed and absorbed by those who attend. In the infrequent but not rare instance of a local physician dying by suicide, it is very helpful to have a mental health professional come to meet with the physicians affected by the loss. This

149

might also include a volunteer from the local chapter of the American Foundation for Suicide Prevention who is a survivor of suicide death. This individual can educate the physicians present about what members of the doctor's family might be experiencing and suggest ways in which they can reach out to or be helpful to the family, without being intrusive or inappropriate.

Psychiatrists can also educate their colleagues by writing a blog. Or writing a column in their newsletters. Or writing a letter-to-the-editor that conveys information about mental illness in physicians. Our work is much more than seeing patients in our offices or clinics or hospitals. We are also advocates, who can and should fight against conditions and beliefs that affect the well-being of our doctor colleagues. Practicing psychiatry for many decades has taught me to speak up for my patients who have been silenced by their illness.

It is encouraging to see that an increasing number of doctors are writing and/or speaking out to their colleagues – or even the general public – about their own personal struggles with depression, bipolar illness, drug abuse, and other mental and emotional problems. We must acknowledge them, thank them for their courage and dignity, and recognize their stories as the gifts that they are. Some categorically state that their mission is to save the life of another physician. I urge anyone who has read a first person account of a physician's illness to send that individual a quick thank you by email or a letter. They will appreciate the compliment and that people are listening.

EDUCATING FAMILIES

"As a father and physician myself, her death makes no sense. I've been preoccupied with this since she died 2 years ago. She was the least likely person to commit suicide, there was a narcissism about her. She was also

very perfectionistic. She was so against seeing someone (a mental health professional). When professionals write about suicide, they should describe more than prevention. They need to emphasize how suicide affects so many people. And it has multiple effects on multiple people. It's so hurtful to people who lose a family member to suicide. There is such tunnel vision in those who are planning their suicide. They can't see how their death is going to affect their families and all the people around them. I've been doing a lot of thinking."

The words of Dr. Julius Skinner (pseudonym) whom I interviewed in the spring of 2015. He lost his daughter Claire, a medical student, to suicide.

There are several ways to better inform the spouses, parents, siblings, and children of doctors who are struggling with a psychiatric illness.

Any doctor who reads an article about depression in doctors should make sure that that his or her family members read it. Overkill? Alarming? Inappropriate? My response is an emphatic and loud "Absolutely not!" Informed family members understand the dos and don'ts of living with someone suffering from depression. They are better able to assist and comfort, to know when to ask questions and when to back off. And they are also able to recognize when their loved one needs help. Over the course of my career, I received countless calls from physicians' family members asking me to see their relative.

HOW FAMILIES CAN HELP

When a physician is in treatment, it is important for the psychiatrist (or therapist) to get some understanding of how the doctor's family is feeling about the patient's illness. By asking the patient – and perhaps reading between the lines –one can get some sense of how informed – or uninformed –his or her loved ones might be. If they seem to be struggling, it is a good idea to ask the patient about setting up a session to include the spouse and/or family. This is called "psychoeducation," and its purpose is to explain what their physician loved one is going through, imparting the diagnosis, and explaining the treatment plan. This is especially important in cases of "treatment resistant depression" requiring multiple medication trials, different types of psychotherapy, and perhaps hospitalization or electroconvulsive therapy. A signed release is essential. To preserve clarity, confidentiality and boundaries, these visits must take place with the patient in the room.

Similar to but different from these sessions are those requested by concerned loved ones who need and wish to share their observations and concerns with the doctor's therapist. This so-called "collaborative information" is always helpful. It may explain why, in some cases, treatment seems to have reached an impasse, or why a condition is worsening, and it can be life-saving when the doctor is suicidal but has not acknowledged this in treatment. The intimate others in the patient's life or home are often able to see things that are not always visible in the psychiatrist's office.

Primary care doctors, psychiatrists, psychologists, and clinical social workers who are treating physicians do not routinely meet in person with anyone other than their patient. This is fine, but I believe it is imperative for them to accept phone calls or other messages from frightened loved ones. The flow of information is acceptably unidirectional. The treating physician does not need to disclose anything about his patient but may be greatly assisted in his treatment by informing the patient that "so and so" has called and conveyed the following and noting his reaction.

After Suicide

And there is a place for education after suicide too. What follows are the insights of Dr. Nancy Dunbar, a psychiatrist. She lost her father to suicide when she was a teenager. I spoke with her by telephone on July 24, 2015.

> *"My dad was kind, funny, smart and sweet. He was from a poor single parent home in Philadelphia. He won a lot of awards, academically very sharp, graduated from U Penn meds and became a radiologist. He was 42 when he killed himself. This was January 22, 1972. I was 16. I was told that he had had an earlier episode of depression in college or medical school. And my mother thinks he had a hypomanic episode before too. The summer before he died, he lost his sparkle, he became more and more a shadow of himself. I remember sitting with him one evening and he wasn't making any sense. He was seeing a psychiatrist and he was prescribed medication but I don't know if he was taking it. He hung himself in the basement of his office. My mother found him because she had gone there when he didn't return home from work and he was unreachable by phone.*
>
> *There was an outpouring from his patients after his death. I think it was public knowledge that my father killed himself. I really didn't talk, even with my therapist. But I've looked back now and I think all of those silent appointments were really very helpful. My therapist was an adult who provided constancy without expectations. I recommend that after suicide it's very helpful to do family work, both individually and together as a family. I think that kids who are survivors of a parent's suicide need to have someone making regular contact with them."*

And here is other advice. This is coming from a physician, Dr. Jay Lee, who attended the service of a classmate from medical school who died by suicide. Here are a few sentences that he wrote in the newsletter of his medical association.[52] I spoke with Dr. Lee by telephone on May 4, 2015.

> *"One of our classmates had taken his own life…and so we found ourselves at his memorial. As I sat there I wondered if any of the speakers would have the courage to address the issue of suicide. Fortunately, one of them, a physician, did, and he reminded us that we have a responsibility to care for each other as we do our patients."*

CHAPTER 12
HOW PATIENTS CAN HELP

In Chapter 4 I gave several examples of how patients are affected when they lose their doctor to suicide. Most often it is a painful, confusing and complicated process that is particularly grueling when the patient has had a very long professional relationship with their doctor.

As patients we need to remember two things. First, our doctors are professionals whom we've consulted to help us when we're ill and to keep us well over the long term. They are highly educated and experienced, especially over time and years of practice. We put our trust in them and expect that they have our best interests at heart. Second, they are also like us, ordinary human beings - men and women with the same insecurities and vulnerabilities as others, especially in the professional world. But when we put our lives in their hands, we don't want to think of this. And that is perfectly normal. When we undergo a surgical procedure we are entrusting a whole team of health professionals with our life, and we expect to wake up safely.

In recent years, however, the doctor-patient model has become more collaborative, meaning that patients are more engaged in their treatment and care. We both can and should ask questions and expect direct and honest answers from our doctors. But I also believe that this means we as patients need to be more aware of our doctors feelings and behavior, and if something seems to be awry, we have an obligation to mention it, particularly when we've had a long-term relationship.

If our doctor seems preoccupied, weary, downcast, or forgetful, we need to reach out, not intrusively but with affection. "Are you okay? You seem tired. Please take care of yourself. I care about you." This is no more than we would do for a friend or a colleague at work, and doesn't the physician who's been looking after our needs deserve the same kindness and courtesy?

More than kind, however, a patient's expression of concern could be the wake-up call that ultimately moves a doctor to get help. I have often had new patients who are physicians tell me that "I think what I'm living with is affecting my work. Just last week, one of my patients told me that I seemed kind of burned out and told me to take better care of myself. I was kind of shocked and a bit embarrassed – I didn't realize that it was beginning to show".

Sometimes a simple note thanking the physician for his care and attention is enough to lift his spirits and return his sense of purpose. I know that many doctors save the thank-you and seasonal greeting cards they receive from grateful patients. They may keep them in a desk drawer and re-read a few on those bad days when they're feeling down and struggling with a sense that they're not really helping anyone. Doing that gives them a boost, a brief reprieve from the doldrums. And for physicians who are really quite depressed and suicidal – but still working - your card could very well be a life-saver.

In the end, patients just need to remember that their doctors are not only extremely dedicated, caring, and great at what they do but also human beings, who may be struggling with the same fears, doubts, stresses – and, yes, mental or emotional problems – that can affect the rest of us.

Part Four

Conclusion

CONCLUSION

I hope that this book is a beginning, not an ending. I hope that the insights recorded here – especially the stories of survivors – will be of help to readers who are trying to grasp the shock and heartache that surround physician suicide. I have tried to distill and integrate what we do know about the psychological vulnerabilities of doctors, their personalities, their proneness to depression or other psychiatric disorders and the many risk factors that come together in a frenzied rush and propel that desperate final act. And yet, every individual is unique, as is every death. In my mind, this is why the narratives in this book, the observations and memories of so many loved ones captured here, are priceless. They are a window into the minds and souls of those whom we've lost. A welcome departure from the cold statistics of suicide.

At the end of the day, even if we have a better understanding of the reasons for a particular physician's suicide, we remain unsettled. The "why" questions may have been answered, or at least partially, but we are still left with such a heavy feeling of loss and regret. We don't want the person to have died – and we don't want him to have died by his own hand. I like to believe that even if we could magically erase the stigma associated with suicide we would still feel this way. And this may be because almost all suicide deaths occur alone. I've never heard anyone ever say that when their time comes, they hope they are all alone. Do not most people have some sort of death bed fantasy of being surrounded by family and/or caring friends when they take their last breath? Do not most loved ones keeping a vigil with their dying relative hope they will be in the room at that very moment, not in the cafeteria or the bathroom or asleep in an adjacent cot. Most obituaries even include such an image for the reader to behold and to feel good about, that she was not alone at the end of her life, her family was there. It just doesn't seem fair that this isn't granted to those who die by suicide.

I hope too that this book is a wakeup call for doctors on the edge. Call someone. Make that phone call that can save your life. The National Suicide Prevention Lifeline number is 1-800-273-8255. One of the hallmarks of suicidal despair is an intractable feeling of being friendless and all alone. It goes with the territory. Every suicidal physician I've treated who is now on the mend and regaining hope looks back and cannot believe how alone and estranged they felt at that point of desperation. It is like night and day, such a bold contrast to how they feel when they're well again. This is why so many of the people I interviewed for this book are fiercely committed to suicide prevention. They believe in their hearts that doctors do not have to die like this. They need to recognize when they're not coping and get help, help that works.

I also hope that the research I've done for this book will stimulate others who are interested in physician suicide. My approach has been qualitative and exploratory – I've used an interview technique that has been semi-structured and my goal has been to uncover hunches, motives or opinions that individuals close to doctors might have. I've looked for themes, trends and patterns in a quest to get at the reasons why physicians kill themselves. My finding that there is a significant minority of doctors who die by suicide without ever receiving any kind of help is I believe novel, and chilling. Perhaps a quantitative researcher will proceed from here and conduct a large survey of physicians (or physician loved ones) to collect data that are measurable and more scientifically rigorous. This could lead to more accurate ways of understanding this phenomenon and robustly contributing to the suicide prevention movement. And this may lead to much needed information on several other variables that we really know very little about that I alluded to at the beginning of this book: age, race, ethnicity, gender, marital status, sexual orientation and gender identity, medical specialty and more. How do these factors put us at risk and how do they protect us?

In the final chapter of our book "Touched by Suicide: Hope and Healing After Loss" Carla Fine and I wrote the following:

> *Our mission in writing this book is to speak candidly about suicide, a subject that for too long has been disregarded and unmentioned in our society. The real voices of people whom we interviewed, and others whose identities we have disguised, are gifts to all of us. Each one of their stories is both unique and universal, and creates a kinship and bond that helps ease our feelings of separateness and isolation.*

I feel the same way as I conclude this book more than a decade later. If anything, I feel more communal – that this challenge, saving the lives of physicians, requires building bridges and cooperative work. This means, at minimum, linking the expertise and dedication of trained professionals of many stripes and the words and actions of the many courageous grieving individuals who have poured out their hearts on these pages. We must continue to be candid and rigorous – and we must keep talking about a subject that, sadly, is not going away. When that day comes, and it will, we can be quiet.

Notes

[1] Swift, Pam, *Doctor's Orders: One Physician's Journey Back to Self*, Glass Horse Press, 2015.

[2] Jiaquan, Xu, MD; Sherry L. Murphy, B.S.; Kenneth D. Kochanek, M.A.; and Elizabeth Arias, Ph.D. CDC, Data Brief 267, December 2016: "Mortality in the United States," 2015.

[3] Sinha, P. "Why do doctors commit suicide?" *New York Times* September 4, 2014.

[4] Myers, M. "The stresses that put doctors at risk," *New York Times* September 5, 2014.

[5] Ofri, D. "Tyranny of Perfection," *Slate*, September 25, 2014.

[6] Reprinted with permission from Myers. M.F. and Gabbard, G.O. *The Physician as Patient: A Clinical Handbook for Mental Health Professionals*, American Psychiatric Publishing, Inc., 2008. All Rights Reserved.

[7] Greenspon, T.S. "Is there an antidote to perfectionism?" http://onlinelibrary.wiley.com/doi/10.1002/pits.21797/full.

[8] Center for Clinical Interventions, http://www.cci.health.wa.gov.au/.

[9] Myers, M.F. "Dr. Control," *Physician's Money Digest*, 2002.

[10] Halperin, Alex, "My brother's life, unraveled," *Salon*, March 12, 2013.

[11] Heckel, Sally, "Unspeakable," http://unspeakablethefilm.com/filmmaker.html.

[12] Joiner, Thomas, *Why People Die by Suicide*, Harvard University Press, 2005.

[13] Jonsen, Albert R. *The Birth of Bioethics*, Oxford University Press.

[14] Carroll, A.E. "Silence is the Enemy for Doctors Who Have Depression," *New York Times*, January 11, 2016.

[15] "A lonely battle," *British Columbia Medical Journal*, 1999, 41(2):66.

[16] Baird, M., and Claxton, E. *He Wanted the Moon: The Madness and Medical Genius of Dr. Perry Baird, and His Daughter's Quest to Know Him*, Crown Publishers, 2015, page 56.

[17] Sontag, S. *Illness as Metaphor*, Farrar, Straus and Giroux, New York, 1978, page 3.

[18] Fine, C. *No Time to Say Goodbye: Surviving the Suicide of a Loved One*. Doubleday, New York, 1997, p 25.

[19] Etkind, M. *Or not to be. A Collection of Suicide Notes*, Riverhead Books, NY, 1997.

[20] Tomkins, A. "Mad doctors? The significance of medical practitioners admitted as patients to the first English county asylums up to 1890", *History of Psychiatry* 23, no. 4 (2012): 437-453.

[21] Legha, R.K. "A History of Physician Suicide in America," *Journal of Medical Humanities*, 2012, 33:219–244.

[22] Scoggin, K. "Last Glimmer of Day," http://www.hawkhouseproductions.com/last-glimmer-of-day/.

[23] Knopf, S. A. "Suicide among American physicians," *New York Medical Journal*, 1923, *117*, 84-87.

[24] Fine, C. "When Physicians Die By Suicide," videotape, produced by Myers, M.F., Biomedical Communications, St. Paul's Hospital, Vancouver, Canada, 1998.

[25] Nuland SB. *How We Die: Reflections on Life's Final Chapter.* Alfred A Knopf, New York, 1994, page 151.

[26] American Foundation for Suicide Prevention, "Struggling in Silence: Physician Depression and Suicide," DVD. 2011.

[27] Myers MF. "Physician suicides leave many victims in their wake," *Winnipeg Free Press*, October 1, 2006.

[28] Broyard A. *Intoxicated by my Illness: And Other Writings on Life and Death.* Fawcett Columbine, New York, 1992, page 44.

[29] Fine C. *No Time to Say Goodbye: Surviving the Suicide of a Loved One,* Doubleday, New York, 1997.

[30] Shneidman ES. *Autopsy of a Suicidal Mind,* Oxford University Press, New York, 2004, page 166.

[31] Jamison KR. "To Know Suicide," OP-ED New York Times, August 15, 2014.

[32] "Report of an Independent Inquiry into the Care and Treatment of Daksha Emson MBBS, MRCPsych, MSc and her daughter Freya," www.simplypsychiatry.co.uk/sitebuildercontent/sitebuilderfiles/deinquiryreport.pdf.

[33] Jamison, K.R. *An Unquiet Mind: A Memoir of Moods and Madness,* Vintage Books, 1997.

[34] Jamison, K.R. *Night Falls Fast: Understanding Suicide,* Vintage Books, 2000.

[35] Stanley, I.H.; Rufino, K.A.; Rogers, M.L.; et al. "Acute suicidal affective disturbance (ASAD): a confirmatory factor analysis with 1442 psychiatric inpatients," *Journal of Psychiatric Research*, 2016, 80:97-104.

[36] Jacoby, A. "Felt versus enacted stigma: a concept revisited: evidence from a study of people with epilepsy in remission," *Social Science & Medicine*, 1994, 38(2):269-274.

[37] Halperin, Alex, "My brother's life, unraveled,"*Salon*, March 12, 2013.

[38] Myers, M.F., and Fine, C. *Touched by Suicide: Hope and Healing After Loss*, Penguin/Gotham, New York, 2006, p 252-253.

[39] Scoggin, K. "Last Glimmer of Day," http://www.hawkhouseproductions.com/last-glimmer-of-day/

[40] Myers, M.F. "Physicians Living with Depression," videotape, American Psychiatric Publishing Inc., Washington, D.C., 1996.

[41] Bauman, K.A. "Physician Suicide," *Archives of Family Medicine*, 1995, (4): 672-673.

[42] Lupin, M.H. "Physician suicide – Where the system fails," *British Columbia Medical Journal*, 1997, (3): 126-128.

[43] "Doctors' diagnosis: Depression.," *British Medical Journal*, Volume 326, June 14, 2003.

[44] Melinek, J., and Mitchell, T.J. *Working Stiff: Two Years, 262 Bodies, and the Making of a Medical Examiner*, Scribner, New York, 2014.

[45] Elkins, R. *My Bright Shining Star: A Mother's True Story of Brilliance, Love and Suicide*, Perfect Publishers Ltd., 2014.

[46] Myers, M.F. "It Is With a Heavy Heart That I Write This…" www.psychcongress.com/blog/it-heavy-heart-i-write-…

[47] Cary, C. "Contemplating 'epidemic of physician suicide'," *Louisville Kentucky Courier-Journal*, February 17, 2015.

[48] Wible, P. *Physician Suicide Letters Answered*, Pamela Wible, MD, January 11, 2016.

[49] The John A. Majda, MD Memorial Fund at the UCSD School of Medicine.

[50] "Collateral Damages: The Impact of Patient Suicide on the Psychiatrist". Cited in "Collateral Damages": Preparing Residents for Coping with Patient Suicide", DVD, *Academic Psychiatry*, 2013.

[51] Middleton, J.L. "Today I'm Grieving a Physician Suicide," *Annals of Family Medicine* 2008, 6(3);267-269.

[52] Lee, J. "Physician's suicide prompts introspection, outreach," *American Academy of Family Physicians News*, February 19, 2015.

BIBLIOGRAPHY

PERIODICALS

Andrew, L.B., and Brenner, B.E. "Physician Suicide," http://emedicine. medscape.com/article/806779-overview.

Berman, A.L., and Silverman, M.M. 'Suicide risk assessment and risk formulation Part II: Suicide risk formulation and the determination of levels of risk," *Suicide and Life-Threatening Behavior*, 2014, 44(4): 432-443.

Bostwick, J.M.; Pabbati, C.; Geske, J.R.; et al. "Suicide attempt as a risk factor for completed suicide: even more lethal than we knew," *American Journal of Psychiatry*, 2016, 173(11): 1094-1100.

Center, C.; Davis, M.; Detre, T.; et al. "Confronting depression and suicide in physicians: a consensus statement," *Journal of the American Medical Association,* 289:3161-3166, 2003.

Dyrbye, L.N.; Satele, D.; Sloan, J.; et al. "Ability of the physician well-being index to identify residents in distress," *Journal of Graduate Medical Education* 2014, 6(1):78-84.

Dyrbye, L.N.; West, C.P.; Satele, D.; et al. "Burnout among U.S. medical students, residents and early career physicians relative to the general U.S. population," *Academic Medicine*, 2014, 89(3):443-451.

Gold, K.J.; Sen, A.; Schwenk, T.L. "Details on suicide among US physicians: data from the National Violent Death Reporting System," *General Hospital Psychiatry* 35(1): 45-49, 2013.

Goldman, M.L.; Shah, R.N.; Bernstein, C.A. "Depression and suicide among physician trainees: recommendations for a national response," Viewpoint, *Journal of the American Medical Association Psychiatry* 72(5): 411-412, 2015.

Guille, C.; Zhao, Z.; Krystal, J.; et al. "Web-based cognitive behavioral therapy intervention for the prevention of suicidal ideation in medical interns: a randomized clinical trial," *Journal of the American Medical Association Psychiatry* 72(12):1192-1198, 2015.

Hochberg, M.S.; Berman, R.S. Kalet, A.L.; et al. "The stress of residency: recognizing the signs of depression and suicide in you and your fellow residents," *American Journal of Surgery*, 2013, 205:141-146.

Hurst, C.; Kahan, D.; Ruetalo, M.; et al. "A year in transition: a qualitative study examining the trajectory of first year residents' well-being," *BMC Medical Education*, 2013, 13:96.

Keller, E.J. "Philosophy in medical education: a means of protecting mental health," *Academic Psychiatry*, 2014, 38:409-413.

Kishore, S.; Dandurand, D.E.; Mathew, A.; et al. "Breaking the culture of silence on physician suicide," Discussion Paper, National Academy of Medicine, https://nam.edu/wp-content/uploads/2016/06/Breaking-the-Culture-of-Silence-on-Physician-Suicide.pdf.

Leslie, Q. "Take a look at me now. A Piece of My Mind," *Journal of the American Medical Association*, 313(2):137-138, 2015.

Mata, D.A.; Ramos, M.A.; Bansal, N.; et al: "Prevalence of depression and depressive symptoms among resident physicians," *Journal of the American Medical Association*, 314(22):2373-2383, 2015.

McGuire, T; Moutier, C.; Downs, N.; et al. In response to "Details on suicide among US physicians: data from the National Violent Death Reporting System," *General Hospital Psychiatry* 35 (2013) 448.

Miller, K.L. "Fighting stigma begins at home," Letter-to-the-editor, *Psychiatric News*, Volume 50, No 16, August 21, 2015.

Myers, M.F. "Physician impairment: is it relevant to academic psychiatry?," *Academic Psychiatry*, 2008, 32:39-43.

Myers, M.F. "Stigma and the ailing physician, Part 3," www.psychcongress. com/blogs/michael-myers-MD/stigma-and-ailing-physician-part-3.

Oreskovich, M.R.; Shanafelt, T.; Dyrbye, L.N. "The prevalence of substance use disorders in American physicians," *American Journal on Addictions*, 24:30-38, 2015.

Rotenstein, L.S.; Ramos, M.A.; Torre, M.; et al. "Prevalence of depression, depressive symptoms and suicidal ideation among medical students: a systematic review and meta-analysis," *Journal of the American Medical Association*, 316(21):2214-2236, 2016.

Salles, A.; Cohen, G.L.; Mueller, C.M. "The relationship between grit and resident well-being," *American Journal of Surgery*, 2014, 207:251-254.

Schernhammer, E.S., and Colditz, G.A. "Suicide rates among physicians: a quantitative and gender assessment (meta-analysis)," *American Journal of Psychiatry*, 161:2295-2302, 2004.

Silverman, M.M., and Berman, A.L. "Suicide risk assessment and risk formulation Part I: A focus on suicide ideation in assessing suicide risk," *Suicide and Life-Threatening Behavior*, 2014, 44(4): 420-431.

Slavin, S.J. "Medical Student Mental Health: Culture, Environment, and the Need for Change," *Journal of the American Medical Association,* 316(21):2195-2196, 2016.

PBS "Struggling in Silence: Physician Depression and Suicide," 2008. DVD available from American Foundation for Suicide Prevention.

Suicide Risk Formulation: A Guide for Psychiatrists, produced by the American Association of Suicidology. Washington, D.C., 2009.

West, C.P.; Dyrbye, L.N.; Rabatin, J.T.; et al. "Intervention to Promote Physician Well-being, Job Satisfaction, and Professionalism A Randomized Clinical Trial," *Journal of the American Medical Association Internal Medicine,* 174(4):527-533, 2014.

BOOKS

Chance, S. Stronger than *Death: When Suicide Touches Your Life.* Replica Books, 1992.

Fine, C. *No Time to Say Goodbye: Surviving the Suicide of a Loved One,* Doubleday, 1997.

Gawande, A. *Being Mortal,* Metropolitan Books, Henry Holt and Company, 2014.

Groopman, J. *How Doctors Think,* Houghton Mifflin, 2007.

Kalanithi, P. *When Breath Becomes Air,* Random House, 2016.

Klitzman, R. *When Doctors Become Patients,* Oxford University Press, 2008.

Mandell, H, and Spiro, H. *When Doctors Get Sick,* Plenum, 1987.

Myers, M.F., and Fine, C. *Touched by Suicide: Hope and Healing After Loss*, Gotham/Penguin, 2006.

Myers, M.F., and Gabbard, G.O. *The Physician as Patient: A Clinical Handbook for Mental Health Professionals*, American Psychiatric Publishing, Inc., 2008.

Nathanson, D.L. *The Many Faces of Shame*, Guilford Press, 1987.

Nuland, S.B. *Lost in America: A Journey with My Father*, AA Knopf, 2003.

Ofri, D. *What Doctors Feel: How Emotions Affect the Practice of Medicine*, Beacon Press, 2013.

Peterkin, A.D. *Staying Human During Residency Training*, Fifth Edition, University of Toronto Press, 2012.

Rynearson, E.K. *Retelling Violent Death*, Brunner-Routledge, 2001.

Simon, R.I. *Preventing Patient Suicide: Clinical Assessment and Management*, American Psychiatric Publishing, Inc., 2011.

Solomon, A. *The Noonday Demon: An Atlas of Depression*, Scribner, 2001.

Sotile, W.M, and Sotile, M.O. *The Resilient Physician*, American Medical Association, 2002.

Styron, W. *Darkness Visible: A Memoir of Madness*, Random House, 1990.

Resources

For Immediate Help

National Suicide Prevention Lifeline
1-800-273-TALK (8255)
www.suicidepreventionlifeline.org

Organizations

American Foundation for Suicide Prevention (AFSP)
120 Wall Street
New York, NY 10005
888-333-2377
www.afsp.org

AFSP has resources specific to medical student and physician suicide, especially the aftermath. There is a brief video on suicidal behavior and a toolkit for training programs should a suicide occur. Here is the link: https://afsp.org/our-work/education/physician-medical-student-depression-suicide-prevention/

American Association of Suicidology (AAS)
5221 Wisconsin Avenue, NW
Washington, DC 20015 202-237-2280
www.suicidology.org

AAS has general resources about suicide including a Task Force on Clinician Suicide that is very helpful for mental health professionals who have lost a patient/client to suicide

Accreditation Council for Graduate Medical Education (ACGME)
Suite 2000
401 North Michigan Avenue
Chicago, IL 60611
Telephone: 312.755.5000
www.acgme.org

The ACGME is deeply committed to physician health and well-being. Here is the link to recent information on symposia and initiatives. This includes a recent collaboration with the National Academy of Medicine: www.acgme.org/What-We-Do/Initiatives/Physician-Well-Being

American Medical Association
AMA Plaza
330 N. Wabash Ave., Suite 39300
Chicago, IL 60611-5885
www.ama-assn.org

There are several sections helpful for physicians: physician health, AMA Alliance (for MD families), Women Physicians, Minority Affairs, LGBTQ issues and more

National Medical Association
8403 Colesville Road
Suite 820
Silver Spring, MD 20910
202-347-1895
www.nmanet.org

For physicians, medical students and patients of African descent.

American Medical Student Association

45610 Woodland Road – Suite 300

Sterling, Virginia 20166

www.amsa.org

There is a section on student well-being

American Medical Women's Association

1100 E. Woodfield Rd.

Suite 350

Schaumburg, IL 60173

Ph: (847) 517-2801

www.amwa-doc.org

There are many resources for medical students, residents and practicing doctors.

American Academy of Emergency Medicine

www.aaem.org

There is a wellness committee

American College of Emergency Physicians

www.acep.org

There is an annual emergency medicine wellness week

Emergency Medicine Residents Association

www.emra.org

There is a wellness committee

Council of Emergency Medicine Residency Directors (CORD)

www.cordem.org

There is a Resilience Committee

American Society of Anesthesiologists

www.asahq.org

There is a Committee on Occupational Health: Substance Use Disorder (SUD) and a section on ASA Wellness Resources

American College of Surgeons

www.facs.org

There is a Committee on Physician Competency and Health

American Academy of Pediatics

www.aap.org

There is a section on Physician Health and Wellness

American Congress of Obstetricians and Gynecologists

www.acog.org

There is a section for members only on resources for physician wellness

American Academy of Family Physicians

www.aafp.org

There is a position paper on burnout in physicians

Federation of State Medical Boards

www.fsmb.org/policy/advocacy-policy/policy-documents

There is a policy section and documents on impairment in physicians

Federation of State Physician Health Programs

www.fsphp.org

Site for information about 47 state physician health programs in the country

Mayo Clinic Physician Health Center

www.mayoclinic.org/departments-centers/preventive-occupational-aerospace-medicine/physician-health-center

Site for comprehensive health screening and fitness-for-duty evaluations of physicians

Suicide Prevention Resource Center (SPRC)

www.sprc.org

Comprehensive resource site for all information about suicide

Samaritans

www.samaritansnyc.org

Much information about suicide prevention and support groups for those who have lost someone to suicide (survivors)

Black Bile

www.black-bile.com

This resource is dedicated to physicians suffering from depression and those who care about them. Its very appropriate sub-title is "because silence is deadening". There is much information here.

ACKNOWLEDGMENTS

It goes without saying that this book would not have happened without the many individuals quoted on these pages and those whom I also interviewed who are not mentioned by name (or pseudonym) but are a monumental part of this book's foundation. How do you thank selfless people? These are men and women who have asked for nothing more than hope, hope that sharing their loss will save a troubled doctor's life, hope that one less family will have to face the sorrow and pain they have confronted, and hope that something will change in the world of medicine. I thank them for letting me in, for opening up their hearts to me, and for accepting me as a chronicler of their loved one's life and death, and an envoy for their recommendations. The words that come to mind as I struggle to describe this process are reverence, grace, humility and awe.

Some of my many physician patients and their families are captured here too. Their stories are disguised and some are composites. I've had a several decades' long career as a "doctors' doctor" and like all physicians, I continue to learn with each passing day. I thank all of them for teaching me and entrusting me with their care. And I thank them for enriching the readers of this book with what I've shared here.

I thank my dear friend and long time collaborator Carla Fine for writing the Forward to this book. She has been a huge support and muse from the beginning of this project – referring survivors of suicide to me, facilitating introductions, expanding my observational reach and assisting with the publishing journey. Since losing her husband Dr. Harry Reiss to suicide in 1989 she has been unflagging in extending a hand and offering sage counsel to survivors all over the globe. Medical educators and mental health professionals, as well, have enormous respect for her writing and sound advice.

Thanks to Judy Kern, my editor. She has done so much more than given this work its flow and editorial polish. She also posed big questions to me, ones that moved me into different territory that I hadn't considered, and those reflections have resulted in depth and clarity. I'm grateful for her seasoned and expansive vision. Dean Fetzer of GunBoss Books has assisted with all of the finishing touches – editing, copy-editing, book cover design and more. I thank him for his creativity, easy manner and patience.

And thanks to Charles Edwards, my husband and ballast. Although he finds this subject personally tough (and he's not alone!) his abiding respect for me and everyone I've interviewed is crystal clear. I love him for that. I'm very grateful for his generosity when my commitment to this work has encroached upon our time together. His humor about "pay-back time" keeps me grounded.

MICHAEL F. MYERS, MD

Dr. Myers is a Professor of Clinical Psychiatry and Immediate Past Vice-Chair Education and Director of Training in the Department of Psychiatry and Behavioral Sciences at SUNY Downstate Medical Center in Brooklyn, New York. He is also a recent past President of the New York City Chapter of the American Foundation for Suicide Prevention.

He is the author or co-author of seven previous books, including Touched by Suicide: Hope and Healing after Loss (with Carla Fine) and The Physician as Patient: A Clinical Handbook for Mental Health Professionals (with Glen Gabbard, MD). He is a specialist in physician health.

Made in the USA
Middletown, DE
21 January 2018